MANAGEMENT WORKSTATIONS STRATEGIES

FOR

OFFICE PRODUCTIVITY

WILLIAM E. PERRY, CQA

Executive Director
Quality Assurance Institute
Orlando, Florida

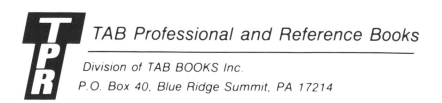

TAB Professional and Reference Books

Division of TAB BOOKS Inc.
P.O. Box 40, Blue Ridge Summit, PA 17214

The pathfinder charting new areas in the Old West was frequently killed, while the pioneer following in the footsteps of the pathfinder received the credit for discovering new lands This book is dedicated to the computer pathfinders whose work builds the base on which current managers' capabilities and productivity is enhanced through the computer-based workstation.

FIRST EDITION
FIRST PRINTING

Copyright © 1987 by TAB BOOKS Inc.
Printed in the United States of America

Library of Congress Cataloging in Publication Data

Perry, William E.
Management workstations.

Includes index.
1. Management—Data processing. 2. Business—Data
processing. I. Title.
HD30.2.P47 1987   658'.05   87-1903
ISBN 0-8306-2833-9

Questions regarding the content of this book
should be addressed to:

Reader Inquiry Branch
Editorial Department
TAB BOOKS Inc.
P.O. Box 40
Blue Ridge Summit, PA 17214

Contents

Introduction

This book is designed to help you, the manager, cope with rapidly changing technology. Strategies are provided to make it easier for you to use the workstation to improve your personal productivity, and to help you develop the methods to be successful at using the workstation to fulfill your day-to-day responsibilities.

A few years ago the workstation was considered a toy of the technician; today it is becoming commonplace in many organizations; and tomorrow the manager without a workstation will be excluded from mainstream decision-making. Concepts that few dared to imagine a few years ago are a reality today. The technology is changing so rapidly that the dreams of today will become realities tomorrow. The workstation will become the vehicle that unleashes office productivity.

In the end, the only successful strategy for mastering the workstation is to become a "believer." Nothing succeeds like success. The first step in using a new technology is the most difficult; the second comes easier. This book is designed to help you survive the impediments and become the master of the workstation technology.

The objective is to provide you with a series of actions which will prevent you from having problems with your workstation. On the other hand, you should be realistic enough to recognize that problems will occur. For this purpose, a Problem Diagnostic Appendix has been added to this book.

The Problem Diagnostic Appendix provides a series of 38 diagnostic programs to help you solve the more common workstation problems. The appendix provides an explanation of how to identify, document, and solve these most common workstation problems. You should keep this appendix near your workstation so you can refer to it whenever a problem occurs.

In this book, the manager's workstation is defined as the means used to access and utilize information. This might take the form of a keyboard and a display used to communicate with the corporate computer, or a microcomputer using an off-the-shelf software spreadsheet program that has the capability to communicate with other microcomputers, or a variety of other configurations, including telephones, designed to aid the manager in performing day-to-day work tasks.

Chapter 1

Workstation Use Is Mandatory, Not Optional

The one item that will not exist in the office of the future is the manager who cannot operate his or her own workstation.

In the early 1900s, the telephone was introduced to the business scene. Many managers felt uncomfortable using this new technology, preferring to write letters and visit colleagues and customers. Others quickly grabbed onto this new technology and began using it to conduct their day-to-day business.

Within a few years, the accelerating pace of business required decisions to be made more rapidly. The managers using telephones were able to call their colleagues for information and to make quick decisions. Those managers who could not be reached by telephone because they fought using this new technology were slowly squeezed out of the decision-making process of their organization. These managers became obsolete in the business world that began relying on the telephone.

The use of the managerial workstation closely parallels the introduction of the telephone. When first introduced, the workstation appeared to be the toy of the technician, and then the equipment of the clerical staff. Eventually, more and more managers began experimenting with this new toy and found that it significantly increased their personal productivity. Part of this productivity gain is associated with a more rapid and effective means of transferring information among one's business colleagues.

Electronic mail and electronic conferencing enable many decisions to be made without the need for formal meetings or informal one to one discussions.

Decisions and concurrence among managers can be obtained much more quickly through the use of communication facilities.

Workstation is a fancy name for a small computer connected to a telephone line that has some special capabilities. To be considered a workstation, the facility must have these capabilities:

- It can receive messages when unattended.
- It can store data electronically.
- It can process data via computer programs.
- It can transmit messages to other facilities and/or people with like capabilities.

An Apple computer or IBM PCjr tied to a communication line could be a workstation. It is the use of electronic equipment to fulfill day-to-day responsibilities, however, not the hardware and software, that turn the above four capabilities into a workstation.

HOW CAN I MASTER THE WORKSTATION?

Very few people are excited about change, but sometimes there is no choice. If you have, are getting, or know you will be getting a workstation, what should you do? The answer is as simple as 1, 2, 3:

1: Convince yourself (and really believe) that workstations are coming and that they will help you personally. The next section of this chapter provides you with the ammunition for belief.

2: Learn the workstation survival strategies. You don't need to be a mechanic to drive a car. What you do need is "street smarts" to utilize this new facility effectively.

3: Develop an action plan and follow it. A ten-step action plan is proposed at the end of this chapter, and then described in detail in the following ten chapters. This book provides the plan—you provide the action!

WORKSTATION FACTS OF LIFE

The advantages and disadvantages of workstations are being debated in management suites throughout the world. Those favoring workstations argue that the access to information sources and people, coupled with the processing capabilities, make workstations a necessity. The anti-workstation crowd argues that the decisions made by management are based on data generally not available to the workstation. For example, many business decisions are made on economic and industrial trends, which are not readily available to the current generation of workstations.

The question of when to acquire a workstation should not be an emotional decision. The facts should support and substantiate that the workstation is needed, or it should not be acquired.

In evaluating the worth of the workstation, let's look at a few facts that build the case for managers using workstations:

FACT 1: A recent survey of U.S. office practices showed that 400 billion paper documents are generated per year, and that this number is growing at a rate of 70 billion documents per year.

Many organizations are drowning in a sea of paperwork. Faster printers and photocopying machines only produce more paper more quickly. They do not get at the root of the problem. Much of the information produced is redundant, and much of it is out of date when it arrives at the user's desk. The workstation eliminates the need for the preparation of many documents, as well as the duplication of those documents for distribution.

FACT 2: Travel accounts for two percent of the budget of many organizations and many managers expend 10-25 percent of their time traveling to and from business meetings.

Much of the travel is related to information transfer. Managers who need to obtain, or impart, information feel it necessary to visit and interact with other managers. Office automation studies show that workstations can reduce travel costs and travel time by 40-60 percent.

FACT 3: Although factory automation continues to show significant productivity gains year by year, the productivity increase of the white-collar staff has been minimal during the past decade. At the same time, the white-collar work force is growing, while the blue-collar work force is diminishing.

Many office tasks are still performed in the same manner they were performed a decade ago. Few managers have significantly improved their methods of document preparation, filing, retrieval, analysis, or interchanging of information in the last decade. These tasks remain very time-consuming and are poorly practiced by too many managers.

Automation offers a great potential for increasing office productivity. Because the workstation is the tool of the individual manager, it is the key to unlocking a manager's potential increase in productivity.

FACT 4: The workstation adds new capabilities. Many people view the workstation as a means of performing the work faster, but not smarter. However, the workstation is capable of performing tasks which could not be performed by an individual without the workstation capability. For example, some of the analysis tasks now possible with spreadsheet software would be impractical to perform manually.

The workstation can provide you with an entire staff ready to analyze and process information faster, using new and more effective methods.

FACT 5: Microcomputers can teach you how to process information using the workstation capabilities.

The difficulty in learning to use the workstation effectively is frequently cited as a major impediment to its use. Data processing professionals indicate that high skills are needed to use the computer, making any attempt intimidating. Most workstation systems include manuals and on-line prompting to aid learning to help you make corrections when you do something wrong. Users learn quickly through mistakes because they have the opportunity to make the error and have it caught by the workstation capabilities. This immediate feedback helps you adjust your procedures to eliminate future errors of the same type.

There is too much unnecessary worry about being unable to master workstation processing. By using all of the workstation capabilities you can become proficient much quicker than most managers believe is possible.

The facts just discussed are designed to demonstrate the need for you to use a workstation. The microcomputer myths should not impede your use of workstations. Many of these myths are fostered by the nonparticipants to justify not using workstations. Let's see how badly you need a workstation in your job.

Workstation Self-Assessment Exercise

You will only be successful at using a workstation when you want to be successful. In psychological terms, this is called ownership. The concept is readily apparent to anyone with a teenage child of driving age. If that teenager drives the parents' car, then the car belongs to the parents and so do all the problems associated with the car. If the tire goes flat, it is the parents' obligation to fix it; if the engine stops working, it is the parents who must fix it; and if the tires need air or the oil must be changed, it is the parents' responsibility to get those things done. This is because the parents own the car, not the child. If, however, the child owns the car instead of parent, the child must do those functions necessary to keep the car working, because it is the child's accepted responsibility.

When a workstation belongs to you, it becomes your responsibility to use it effectively and take care of it. When the workstation is imposed on you through outside decisions, then the responsibility for the effective use of the workstation belongs to management, not you. When people don't want a workstation, they develop a "show me" attitude, and the self-fulfilling prophecy of failure occurs.

A self-assessment exercise to evaluate your need for a workstation is shown in Fig. 1-1. This checklist is a series of questions to ask yourself. Based on your responses to this brief self-assessment, you can judge your need for a workstation.

Evaluating the Self-Assessment Exercise Results

The self-assessment exercise is designed so that "yes" responses indicate

Item	Response			
	Yes	No	N/A	Comments
1. Do you need information contained in the organization's centralized database?				
2. Do you have to look up telephone numbers before you dial most individuals?				
3. Do you frequently have trouble retrieving documents in your personal filing system?				
4. Do you frequently send out more than one copy of a document?				
5. Do you write draft letters and memorandums in longhand?				
6. Does your organization have an electronic mail capability?				
7. Do you prepare financial worksheets on a regular basis? (A worksheet is a sheet with both rows and columns.)				
8. Do you have difficulty getting messages to or from your business colleagues?				
9. Does your job involve the analysis of factual information?				
10. Do you frequently have to rearrange or analyze information presented to you in formal reports?				
11. Do you spend many minutes a day filing and retrieving information?				
12. Do you keep a personal appointment calendar?				
13. Does your job involve mathematical calculations?				
14. Do you frequently prepare lists of work to perform?				
15. Are you dependent upon other people to store and retrieve information needed in the performance of your job?				
16. Do you need information from files and documents while you talk to colleagues on the telephone?				

Fig. 1-1. Evaluating the need for workstation processing.

potential uses of the workstation, and "no" responses show activities that can best be performed manually. An indication of your need for workstation capabilities can be determined by accumulating the number of "yes" responses on the other self-assessment exercise and using Table 1-1 to interpret the results.

This self-assessment exercise is not a high-precision evaluation. On the other hand, it separates those who desperately need workstations from those who can probably survive quite well without them. If you need a workstation, or have been given one, the rest of the book will help you survive the transition into the 21st century of office technology.

LEARN THE WORKSTATION SURVIVAL STRATEGIES

One of the comforting factors about surviving workstation technology is

Table 1-1. Interpreting the Workstation Self-Assessment Exercise.

Number of Yes Responses	Interpretation of Frequency of Yes Responses
0-4	'You do not appear to be one who will benefit initially from the use of the workstation. It might provide some help, but your current job function and/or organizational capabilities do not appear to warrant installing a workstation.
5-8	You will receive some benefit from a workstation. Initially you might not need full workstation processing capabilities. However, as you begin to utilize the workstation, you should note increased benefits over time.
9-12	You will benefit significantly from the installation of the workstation. Benefits should be immediate and grow rapidly. Within a short period of time you will wonder how you survived without the assistance of a computer-based workstation.
13-16	You have needed a computer-based workstation for a long time, and probably know it. Most likely, your personal progress in your organization in inhibited by the lack of workstation capabilities. The addition of a workstation will significantly improve your productivity and free up time for you for more important activities.

that you are not alone. The challenge is being faced by hundreds of thousands of managers in the performance of their job function. If might be comforting to know that most of today's managers would be just as happy without a workstation—at least in the beginning.

The learning curve you will travel through in using workstation technology involves four distinct phases, as follows (see Fig. 1-2 for an illustration of the learning curve):

Phase 1: Workstation Experimentation. A workstation is a tool, a capability, and a resource to the manager. In some ways it is an extension of your own analytical capabilities, but at the same time it is a link to information and people. It is difficult to restructure the methods by which work is performed. Therefore, it is necessary to go through an experimentation phase, attempting to utilize the new technology.

During the experimentation phase, the cost and risks of using workstation technology are minimized, but so are the benefits. During this time, you will experiment with your new "toy." For example, if you cannot remember how a hand calculator performs arithmetic, a simple problem such as three plus four might be entered so that you can experiment and find out how to use the calculator for arithmetic. The same process occurs in workstation learning. A few unimportant or simplified tasks are experimented with, just to learn how the basic functions of the workstation are performed.

Phase 2: Workstation Use Causes Problems. The early confidence gained by performing "toy" tasks will be quickly eroded as you begin to use the workstation for real business purposes. You will find out that the workstation is a very effective teacher, but very unforgiving. You either do it exactly by the rules or you will be in trouble.

This phase in which you encounter problems is like your youth. Although

6

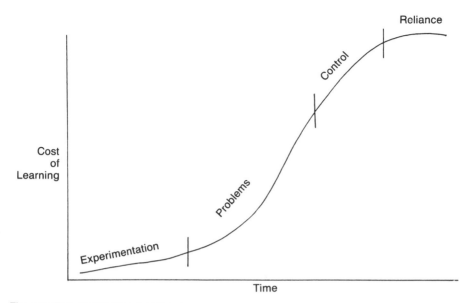

Fig. 1-2. The workstation learning curve.

parents can warn and caution about life's problems, most youths must learn from experience. These painful lessons are well taught, but not without grief. You will experience the same agony as you increase workstation usage. For example, you can be told about the need to save input data on a regular basis, but the first time that six or eight hours of your personal processing are lost due to a power failure or some other computer-related glitch, you will finally realize why it is so important to save computer data at regular intervals. (This concept will be covered in Chapter 8.)

The problems phase is common to everyone. However, try to get through the problems phase as quickly as possible. Most of this book is directed at solving the problems and moving through this phase to the next phase, in which control enters the workstation processing scene.

Phase 3: Workstation Control. Control is often viewed as an impediment to getting work done. The control imposed by centralized data processing groups often appears unnecessary. The workstation provides the manager with the opportunity to forgo the central data processing controls, and thus might appear to make the workstation very advantageous. However, the problems phase prepares you for the need for workstation control. Procedures and methods that might appear unnecessary when you first acquire the workstation will be viewed as essential for survival by the end of the problems phase. Controls make using a workstation easier and more fun because you don't have a lot of operational problems.

Most of the controls will be provided with the workstation capabilities. Some are automatic, but many are manually initiated. For example, the decision to duplicate and save computer data is normally a manually initiated control. The use of these controls will reduce your problems and enable you to rely more upon the integrity of your processing results.

Phase 4: Workstation Reliance. Once the controls are in place and working, you can rely upon the results produced by the workstation. This final phase of the learning curve is the most satisfying. At this point, you will be well on the road to improved personal productivity.

At this point, the way you do work, and the time allocation to work tasks, will change significantly. More on this later in the book.

Tools for Survival

Surviving the introduction of the workstation in your company will require the rethinking of how you perform your job function. Unfortunately, most organizations throw their managers into the "lion's pit" of technology with little or no training. For many managers it is a sink or swim situation when the technology is thrust upon them.

Surviving is essential to one's mental and financial health. This book provides the following survival tools to managers:

1: Insight into Workstation Technology. The first two chapters of this book give a behind-the-scenes look at the workstation environment. These chapters explain how the workstation functions, what is involved in mastering the skills needed to operate the workstation effectively, and the benefits that you should derive from using the workstation.

2: Workstation Survival Rules. Ten rules are given to survive in the managerial suite equipped with a workstation. Chapters 3 through 12 explain how to use each of the ten survival rules. Armed with these workstation strategies, you can survive the best that technology can throw at you, and even prosper beyond your expectations.

3: Workstation Performance Appraisal. All managers need to know whether they are getting their money's worth or whether they are being snowed by the technicians. The last chapter of the book (Chapter 13) provides a method to help you evaluate the effectiveness of your workstation performance. You would hate to master a second-class product. Once you have learned how to survive, you will want the best workstation facility that money can buy in order to maximize your personal productivity.

One more survival rule is needed, but it cannot be provided in this book. It is the desire to master workstation technology, and to take sustained action to fulfill that objective. This book explains how to survive, but cannot give the will to survive. That must come from within. However, the survival rules given here will support sustained action by minimizing the effort required to master the workstation, and help reduce the intimidating effects of advanced computer technology.

If you need it—welcome to the world of workstation technology.

DEVELOP A WORKSTATION PLAN OF ACTION

Change is difficult for anybody. Even changes that we desire come hard. As a youth, when you went from walking to bicycling, the transition involved many falls and bruises. The goal of bicycling, however, appeared worth the agony of mastery. It is easier to do nothing than to do something. It is easier to fail than to succeed. It is often easier to explain why you do not do something than to do it.

It is important to recognize that moving from manual processing to workstation processing will be difficult, both creatively and technically. However, the technical mastery is often easier than the creative mastery of the wonderful world of workstation technology.

Survival is dependent upon two things. The first is the mental desire and the sustained interest necessary to master the new technology. In learning how to ride a bicycle you really had to want to ride the bike in order to suffer the pain of learning. The second is learning techniques that enable you to survive the process. In mastering bike-riding, two of the techniques were to let an adult help support you until you mastered the peddling skills, and, if trouble appeared, to plant your feet firmly on the ground so the bike wouldn't teeter out of control.

The lessons learned by the workstation pioneers provide an action plan. The stacked bodies of the nonsurvivors attest to the fact that planning is needed. The dropout rate of microcomputer workstation users exceeds 20 percent. If those who are barely participating are added, it reveals that almost half of the managers using workstations are not successful.

Etched out of the experience of the survivors are the ten actions listed on Fig. 1-3. You need to adopt them as your personal plan of action. Chapters 3 through 12 explain how to implement those actions. The use of these ten actions should make your life significantly easier as you begin using the workstation in your job to aid you in increasing your personal productivity.

Workstation Rules of Thumb

The key points discussed in this book are reiterated as workstation rules of thumb. These rules of thumb will be placed through the book at the point where a new concept is introduced. Keeping them in mind will assist you in utilizing workstation technology effectively. The first rule of thumb follows.

WORKSTATION RULE OF THUMB
If it is going to be, it is up to me. Only "me" can make the workstation work for me!

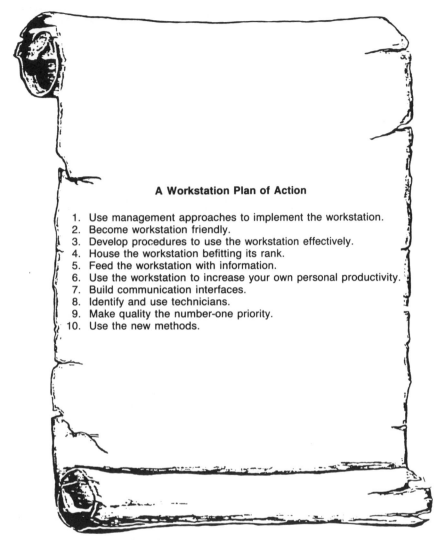

A Workstation Plan of Action

1. Use management approaches to implement the workstation.
2. Become workstation friendly.
3. Develop procedures to use the workstation effectively.
4. House the workstation befitting its rank.
5. Feed the workstation with information.
6. Use the workstation to increase your own personal productivity.
7. Build communication interfaces.
8. Identify and use technicians.
9. Make quality the number-one priority.
10. Use the new methods.

Fig. 1-3. A workstation plan of action.

Chapter 2

Customizing
Your Workstation

A plan is the shortest distance between a desire and a reality. A plan is the basis for fulfilling the motto "If it is going to be—it is up to me."

This chapter explains what a workstation is or could become. It will help you determine what job responsibilities should be performed on the workstation. The chapter describes how your workday will be restructured as you incorporate workstation processing to complete tasks.

For clerical personnel, workstations are carefully designed and delivered. Procedures are developed and the clerical staff are instructed in the utilization of their workstations. Many of the workstations are directly connected to the central computer. These applications are frequently called "slave" stations because the user has little control over how the terminals are used.

The manager's workstation is much more personal. It becomes an extension of the management function. This aspect of the organization has not been reduced to a series of computer applications performed routinely. In many instances, the manager's workstation is a resource which must be utilized through personal initiative.

Some of the workstation capabilities are general in nature and will be used by most managers. These include such facilities as electronic mail, voice communication, and financial data analysis. Other capabilities, such as database storage and word processing are there to assist in the fulfillment of managerial functions, and must be adapted for specific situations.

11

UNMASKING THE WORKSTATION

"Workstation" is a new term used frequently, but rarely defined. A work-station is normally pictured in magazines as an ultramodern office area garnished with electronic gear and highlighted by a cathode-ray display tube. Many look like this, but most are much more plainly "dressed." Although the ubiquitous tube is a mainstay in the workstation complex, the types of equipment configurations are almost unlimited.

The office management staff likes to describe the use of workstations as the office of the future. Data processing personnel view workstations as computer terminals. Others think of their desk, chair, and other office furniture as their workstation.

The workstation should be called the "electronic workstation." However, just as electronic data processing has dropped the electronic label, so has the workstation. The workstation, as it is commonly known, represents the use of electronic and voice equipment to assist an individual in the performance of a job.

Not all workstations have voice capabilities, but they should, for managers. The workstation with voice is technically referred to as the integrated voice/data terminal (IVDT). The objective is to integrate all the information-processing aids into a single unit.

The workstation is defined as automated processing capabilities provided to assist an individual in fulfilling job responsibilities. It can include data processing, word processing, telecommunications, graphics, hardware, software, and the procedures relating to the interactive use of these capabilities.

Workstations must be configured for their users. The options available for the configuration of a workstation are as varied as those provided the purchaser of an automobile. The actual workstation configuration provided to a manager can be structured to suit any job responsibilities.

Most organizations provide the basic workstation framework. At a minimum, this will include:

- A method for entering data into the workstation.
- Computer storage and processing capability.
- A method for outputting data from the workstation.

Beyond these basic capabilities, the size and flexibility of the workstation is almost unlimited. In addition, today's restrictions will be tomorrow's capabilities. Technology is moving so rapidly that the capabilities are rarely limited by the technical capabilities of the equipment. For example, teleconferencing is a logical extension of the manager's workstation.

WORKSTATION RULE OF THUMB
The workstation capabilities available to today's manager are only limited by the imagination of the individuals designing the workstation.

COMMON WORKSTATION CAPABILITIES

Workstation capabilities are the basic building blocks used by workstation designers. Workstation architects all use the same "clay," but they can mold that clay into an almost infinite variety of workstation configurations. It is helpful to the managers to understand these components so that they can assist in molding their personal workstations.

Listed below are the major components of a workstation. (Note that some components are hardware devices, others are concepts, most of which are implemented through software.)

Word Processing. Systems are designed to assist in the preparation of reports, documents, and letters. Capabilities include document structuring such as automatic heading and page numbering, automatic columnar totaling, verification of correct spelling, automatic rearrangement of material when words are modified, insertion of prepared material into documents, word searches or correction or change, and reproduction of documents.

Dictation. Managers can dictate onto workstation electronic media and then have that dictation automatically transcribed to printed format. Within the near future, dictation will be directly to equipment and transcribed to printed format without human intervention.

Facsimile. Hard-copy documents can be transmitted from one location to another in electronic format. A document entered at one location is reproduced in the same format at a remote location.

Optical Character Readers (OCRs). This equipment can read information contained on hard-copy documents. In some instances the type and structure of the letters must be standardized in order to be read by OCR equipment.

Directory. Lists of names, telephone numbers, mailing addresses, and other data about people are maintained for local storage and retrieval. It usually works using key words, such as a person's last name or city.

Two-Line Capability. This permits conferencing calls between yourself at your workstation, and two or more other individuals.

Calendar. A storage and retrieval facility is provided to keep track of appointments, due dates, and checkpoints. Data can be retrieved on a daily, weekly, or monthly basis.

Alarm. This is an audible or visual reminder of an appointment. It can be set for a few minutes before appointments to allow time to reach the meeting area.

Calculator. A numeric keypad or keyboard, this is to perform mathematical computations.

Electronic Files. Documents are stored and retrieved in electronic media.

Databases. Pieces or groups of data are stored in a format that makes them readily retrievable using different data access keys. For example, employee information might be retrievable by employee number, social security number, department, job skill, or any other data attribute desired by the manager. Note that in many instances the same database can be shared by multiple workstations.

Electronic Mail. Documents are moved to different locations through predetermined distribution codes or addresses.

Intelligent Copiers. Such reproduction equipment can perform analysis and rearrangement during the copy process.

Printers. These machines can reproduce information from electronic media onto paper.

Microfilm/Microfiche Readers. Such equipment can select and display information stored on microfilm or microfiche.

Electronic Mail Box. Information directed to specific individuals is stored until that individual is ready to retrieve it.

Automatic Telephoning (i.e., Telephone Directory). This equipment can retrieve telephone numbers and automatically dial those numbers, and redial as often as necessary until a response is obtained. Dialing can occur through the use of key words such as "boss" rather than by telephone number.

Communication Networks. This provides the capability to transmit and receive information from other workstations and computers.

Software Packages. The computer processing capabilities of the workstation can perform almost unlimited tasks through the acquisition of the necessary processing programs. These libraries of processing programs provide the manager with the support systems needed to fulfill job responsibilities.

The equipment providing these capabilities needs to be integrated into traditional office equipment, such as bookshelves, filing cabinets, and telephone equipment. The proper mix and structure of furniture and equipment is important to ensure the effective use of the workstation. The physical structuring of the workstation will be described in Chapter 6.

These facilities represent a shopping basket of capabilities for structuring the workstation. The work challenges of the manager must be identified, and the appropriate elements assembled into a workstation specifically designed for that individual. The customization of the workstation is an important part of ensuring its effective use.

```
┌─────────────────────────────────────────────────────┐
│           WORKSTATION RULE OF THUMB                  │
├─────────────────────────────────────────────────────┤
│                                                     │
│        The structuring of a workstation is          │
│        equivalent to strolling down the aisle       │
│        of a workstation super-market and            │
│        placing into your workstation shop-          │
│        ping basket the specific capabilities        │
│        needed to support your job                   │
│        responsibilities.                            │
│                                                     │
└─────────────────────────────────────────────────────┘
```

CUSTOMIZING FOR A MANAGER

A workstation is not a single thing but, rather, a customized processing capability for a manager. It must fit like an old shoe in order to meet a specific manager's need. The better the fit, the more effective the workstation becomes.

This customization process can be viewed from two perspectives. The first perspective includes the problems that managers need to solve in order to boost their productivity. These are the generalized challenges facing most managers. The second perspective is the identification of the specific problems facing you. This involves creating a processing baseline of the work you are currently performing to show the areas where a workstation could be most helpful.

What Problems Need Solving?

An obvious question to ask when confronted with a decision regarding acquiring a workstation is, "How can I use a workstation?" The answer to that question must relate to solving your current managerial problems, or providing better methods of performing your tasks. Unless the workstation developers can properly answer the manager's question, the justification for the workstation will be questionable.

The following examples show a few of the problems most managers now face, which can be eliminated or improved through the effective use of a managerial workstation:

• Telephone tag—Person A calls Person B, but Person B is away from his desk. Later, Person B calls A, but now A is away from his desk. When A returns to his desk and calls B, B is away, and on and on the tag goes. When the contact is finally made by telephone, it might be too late, or the answer might have been found through another source.

• Scheduling mazes—When a meeting between A and B is to occur, it becomes necessary to find a free time on both A's and B's calendar and schedule the meeting for that time. When A, B, and C meet, the task becomes more difficult, and when A, B, C, and D meet it is even more perplexing. Perhaps, to free D's schedule, D must change a meeting with E in order to be free to meet with A, B, and C, which then must be rescheduled with E, and if E was meeting with F and G, people can spend hours scheduling and rescheduling.

15

An age-old story exemplifies this. It explains how for the want of a nail by a shoemaker, the war was lost.

- Frustration of finding information—There are times when people feel they spend their entire life searching for something stored where they thought they could find it when they wanted it. Some people try to solve this problem by having duplicate files, and then find they lose the very same document in both filing systems. In other instances, the document is filed by a third party (e.g., a secretary) and when that person is gone nothing can be found.

- Distribution dilemma—Some people feel that organizations are now dependent upon a copy machine for survival. The question arises about who should get copies, and who should not, but if someone is overlooked they might be upset. Meanwhile, the cost of copying and disseminating goes out of sight. It is sometimes difficult to get the documents you want, and difficult to stop getting those that you do not want.

These are but a few of the problems that managers face every day. All are frustrating, and none appear to be readily solvable without a significantly new concept. That new concept is the workstation.

THE CUSTOMIZATION PROCESS

The customization process begins by developing a workload baseline of your managerial activities. A baseline is an analysis and quantification of the current activities you are performing. The objective of developing the baseline is that the workstation can be fitted to your needs. Until the type and magnitude of your activities is determined through the baseline process, it will be difficult to create the appropriate workstation for you.

Baselines of tasks for managers are not readily available. They need to be established for each manager. The tools for establishing your baseline follow. However, the actual recording of the information is your responsibility. Bite the bullet and do it.

There are two reasons why you, as a manager, should establish a baseline of tasks that you now perform. The first is to identify areas in which workstations would provide you the most benefit. For example, if you spend a large amount of your time retrieving factual information about people, schedules, and events, a workstation directory would be a valuable tool for you to use.

Second, your baseline of time spent on tasks will be significantly changed after the workstation is installed. This initial baseline can be used to demonstrate the value of the workstation in fulfilling your primary job responsibilities. What you should experience is a significant shift from spending large amounts of time on clerical functions such as searching for minor factual data, and using that time for the more important tasks such as planning and organizing.

There are two approaches you can use to establish your workload baseline:

Approach 1—Estimate baseline activities based on your recollection and judgment of the work you do. This requires you to divide your time into groups of baseline activities. Although this method is the quickest approach, it is also the least reliable. In many instances, you might not be able to objectively recognize where and how you spend your time, or in some instances you might be unaware of where your time is being expended.

Approach 2—Record your activities over a predetermined evaluation period. You can select a day, a couple of days, or a week to record specifically how your time is being expended. This requires you to constantly watch your time so that when you change your activity, it can be properly recorded. Some organizations that do this professionally do it through the use of timers. A timer goes off every few minutes and the manager jots down, or records into dictating equipment, what is being done at that precise time. From this, an extrapolation can be made of managerial activities. This second approach is recommended.

The development of a baseline of work activities can be performed by following these three steps:

1: Record the Daily Tasks You Perform in a Log. Each day of the baseline period, you need to record all of the tasks that your perform. It is recommended that a one-week period (i.e., five days) be used to create the baseline. Although there are monthly, quarterly, and annual tasks, they normally take an insignificant part of your time. A week of activities is normally sufficient to identify all of your time-consuming managerial activities.

Figure 2-1 provides a log for recording your tasks. The log includes a place to indicate which day is being recorded. During the day, you should indicate the time that each task commences. Only four pieces of information need be recorded for each event. The time column should indicate when you begin work during the day and conclude at the end of the day. The tasks can be written in any manner that is understandable to the manager.

At the end of the day, the duration in minutes for each task should be calculated. This is the time span between the start of a task and the start of the following task. For purposes of the managerial log, assume no lost time unless it is indicated on the log. Each task should then be classified according to a standardized classification scheme. A suggested scheme for classifying managerial tasks is listed in Fig. 2-2. (Note that the thirteen tasks described on Fig. 2-2 list the activity classifications that are proposed for use in the activity classification column on Fig. 2-1. To make it easier for the manager, a task number could be substituted for the name.) Add other tasks appropriate to your job.

2: Summarize Daily Tasks on a Baseline Period Worksheet. After the log of your baseline tasks has been completed, they should be summarized and transcribed to the Baseline Activities Worksheet (Fig. 2-3). If five days are used in the baseline period, all five columns on Fig. 2-3 will be com-

Day _____		Manager _____	

Time	Task	Duration	Activity Classification

Fig. 2-1. A form to log managerial tasks.

pleted. The total time included for each day's activity should equal the total time worked by the manager.

3: Develop and Use the Baseline Profile. The process of logging managerial tasks is the major effort in creating your baseline. Recording, transcribing and creating the baseline profile are mechanical tasks. At the end of Step 2, all of the needed information is on the Fig. 2-3 worksheet. The information then needs to be totaled horizontally in the total column. The number of minutes or hours in the total column should now equal the amount expended by the manager in the baseline period. These totals must then be converted into percentages to show what percent of the manager's time is spent on which activity. Once the total minutes have been converted into percent, the baseline profile is complete.

The baseline profile can be converted into a bar chart, a pie chart, or a listing of activities. Figure 2-3 shows the profile; however, showing the activities in a graphical format such as a bar or pie chart would make them easier to interpret.

The baseline profile is used to identify areas for potential improvement.

Task #	Task Name	Task Description
1.	Document filing/retrieval	Time expended to place documents in a location for later use, or time expended retrieving documents from the storage area. If a second person does the retrieval for the manager, the manager only records the time involved in making the request.
2.	Data analysis	Time spent analyzing documents. This could include the rearrangement of the sequence, comparison between documents, and other logical analyses that are required for decision-making.
3.	Telephoning	Looking up telephone numbers, dialing, redialing, and talking to individuals.
4.	Reproduction/copy	Time expended going to and from copy machines, time spent copying at machine, and time spent which is primarily copying from one document to another.
5.	Data gathering	Time expended locating information that is not directly available to the manager. Data gathering can be from individuals, from other areas, or using centrally located terminals or repositories of information. Data gathering also includes reading periodicals and documents.
6.	Recording/transcribing	Time expended completing forms, entering data on forms or other documents, and moving data from one form or report to another.
7.	Creating documents	The origination of reports, letters, memos, or other formally recorded documents.
8.	Conferencing/consulting	Meetings with other individuals, such as one-to-one meetings, impromptu meetings, or formally scheduled meetings for a group. Conferencing can occur in one's office, current business location, or in a remote location.
9.	Computing	The performance of mathematical, statistical, and other computational activities. These functions can be performed mentally, using hand-held calculators, or using remote terminal facilities.
10.	Organizing/scheduling/ planning	Time spent in planning work, assigning people to work, scheduling work, and ensuring that work is being properly performed.
11.	Traveling	Time spent going between two or more locations.
12.	Waiting	Time that cannot be productively utilized because of the need to wait for an individual to become available, obtain a response over the telephone, or have some event to occur.
13.	Other	Any task that is not appropriately described in the above twelve tasks. This provides the opportunity for the manager to create special tasks for special conditions.

Fig. 2-2. Common managerial tasks.

	Time Period	1	2	3	4	5	Total	%
Baseline Activity								
1.	Document filing/retrieval							
2.	Data analysis (e.g., rearrange, compare)							
3.	Telephoning							
4.	Reproduction/copy							
5.	Data gathering							
6.	Recording/transcribing							
7.	Creating documents							
8.	Conferencing/consulting							
9.	Computing (e.g., math)							
10.	Organizing/scheduling/planning							
11.	Traveling							
12.	Waiting							
13.	Other (specify):							
	a) _____							
	b) _____							
	c) _____							
	d) _____							
	e) _____							

Fig. 2-3. The baseline activities worksheet.

For example, if you are spending a large part of your time recording and transcribing documents (activity 6) then the workstation should be constructed to help you perform that task more efficiently and economically. On the other hand, if you are spending your time in data analysis (activity 2) and computing (activity 9), an entirely different workstation might be developed to assist you.

The allocation of time among the baseline activities will vary by job function, by management style, and the level of management positions held. For example, middle management does more organizing/scheduling/planning and conferencing/consulting than either first-line supervision or top management. If you were a typical manager (which no one is) a time distribution among the twelve baseline activities is given in Table 2-1.

If you read the personal computer ads, or watch demonstrations, it all looks easy. You might be thinking, "Why do I have to go through all this analysis, why not just get it and use it?" The answer is that you are not getting a simple tool, you are getting a capability which will restructure the way you do your job. This is a *major* change in the way you will operate. Don't treat the challenge lightly. It's like building a house. If you don't spend enough time plan-

Table 2-1. Time Distribution of the Twelve Baseline Activities.

Number	Baseline Activity Name	Time Distribution (in percentage)
1.	Document filing/retrieval	4%
2.	Data analysis	8
3.	Telephoning	13
4.	Reproduction/copy	5
5.	Data gathering	11
6.	Recording/transcribing	5
7.	Creating documents	10
8.	Conferencing/consulting	21
9.	Computing	5
10.	Organizing/scheduling/planning	5
11.	Traveling	9
12.	Waiting	4

ning the house, you will regret it the entire time you live in the house, and unless you want to spend bundles of money you will have to live with your mistakes.

The profile you just created tells you where you need help. Getting help will require you to implement the ten-step plan of action listed in the previous chapter. That plan must become your plan. With it, you have your requirements, the baseline profile, and the steps needed to improve the activities which will make the greatest contribution to improving your personal productivity.

IMPLEMENTING YOUR PLAN OF ACTION

Things that are planned do not happen without follow-through. A plan of action is a plan to create and install the right workstation for you. This plan of action should be initiated by you, or in conjunction with the technician who will oversee the technical aspects of implementation.

Your workstation plan of action should be directed at integrating the workstation into the day-to-day functioning of your job. The objective of the plan is to accomplish that goal with as little effort and pain as possible. At the heart of the proposed plan of action are the ten actions that will be described in the next ten chapters.

Three guidelines you can use in implementing your plan of action are:

1: Use the Experimentation Period to Learn the Workstation Capabilities. You should not rely on the workstation until you become comfortable with the equipment. Time must be scheduled for experimentation before the equipment is relied upon in the performance of your job. It is as much a mistake to use the equipment too soon as it is to wait too long to benefit from the capabilities of the workstation. You need time to become knowledgeable in using the workstation and to customize to your specific needs. This experimentation period normally takes 4-12 weeks, but is necessary for you to master the basic workstation skills.

2: Install Controls Over Workstation Processing. Workstation capabilities provide the opportunity for control, but normally do not require control. One of the best pieces of advice that you can gain is to take advantage of the controls included with the workstation activities and procedures. Control is used in the very broad sense to mean the system of methods and techniques used to ensure the integrity of workstation processing.

3: Use the Workstation Every Day. Once you have learned how the workstation functions, and have incorporated the appropriate control mechanisms into the process, you should use the workstation extensively. It is the key to personal productivity in the 1990s. The managers that begin using workstations today will be tomorrow's heroes. The managers who fight the workstation today might find that they are no longer needed in a year or two.

WORKSTATION RULE OF THUMB
A workstation is not to be loved but, rather, used. The bottom line for using a personal computer is the increases in productivity it allows.

Chapter 3

Action 1: Use a Management Approach to the Workstation

You can solve a technical problem with managerial solutions, but you cannot solve a managerial problem with technical solutions.

This chapter is designed to demonstrate that workstations are for anyone needing faster or more effective information processing. Many of the problems associated with the implementation and operation of workstations are managerial problems requiring managerial solutions. For example, integrating many managers into an effective communication network and automating strategic planning is not a technical problem but, rather, a managerial problem. Although the manager's workstation might technically be ready to operate, the supporting manual systems might not be.

The installation of workstations represents a significant change in the methods by which a manager does business. This chapter explores the behavioral aspects of those changes and suggests strategies to address some of the implementation and usage problems. The chapter explores why some managers have trouble accepting these strategies, and how this can be overcome.

Information processing is a field that has been dominated by technical people for the past three decades. Many of these data processing professionals claim that every organizational problem is solvable by computers. Their hypothesis is that everything is a technical problem which can be solved by technicians. Experience is demonstrating that this is not true.

The computer technicians have performed some outstanding feats during the past three decades, but have not solved all business problems. Problems solvable by technical solutions, such as the automatic processing of payroll, work very well as computerized applications. On the other hand, problems dealing with people generally defy technical solutions. It is in precisely those areas, such as data preparation and output usage, that most of the data processing problems are occurring today.

A self-assessment checklist is provided as a tool to help the manager survive the challenges described in this chapter.

THE NEED FOR MANAGERIAL SOLUTIONS

Computer technology is intimidating to many people. You only need to stand outside a bank and watch the individuals who perform their banking electronically at automatic teller machines, and then look at those who walk inside to a human teller. You will observe technological discrimination between those who will work with machines and those who won't. To make matters even worse, some banks are threatening to put a surcharge on those who bypass the machines to bank with people—a severe form of technical discrimination.

You, as a manager, are the key ingredient to making your workstation work. The technicians can give you a capability, but their role stops at that point. You must ensure that you get the needed capabilities, the needed training, and the needed support. It will be the use of your managerial talents that will decide the degree of success. For example, a financial spreadsheet is merely a matrix of information—it is up to you what you put into the matrix, how to interpret the spreadsheet information, and then how to use that information in solving a business problem. The reason managers haven't used workstations before is because technicians don't know what managers need.

The technically intimidated (a lot of people) tend to feel incompetent when it comes to working with technology. In looking for a technical problem, few of us would raise the hoods of our automobile, peer behind the back of our television set, or propose how to install or modify a workstation. Because we live in an age of specialization, we assume that these technical areas are the exclusive domain of technicians.

Let's examine some of the reasons why the manager's workstation environment has been so slow in evolving:

- Managers do not understand the need to have a workstation installed in their office.
- Workstations are installed in such a manner that they are physically difficult to access and use.
- Workstation hardware and software is not fully tested and is delivered with obvious defects.
- Systems, such as electronic mail, are only partially implemented in the organization.

24

- Funding is inadequate to provide a full-service workstation. Many desired features are not included in the initial installation, which diminishes the usefulness of the equipment.
- Managers are not provided sufficient training to help them master the workstation.
- Operating procedures for the managers are not prepared, or are poorly prepared.
- The benefits expected from workstations are neither documented nor evaluated to demonstrate that they occur.

Management takes the brunt of the criticism for everything in an organization that does not work. Following the "it's management's fault" theme, you can also state the reason workstations don't work is because management is not properly committed and involved in workstations. Although this is a major cause of the ineffective use of workstations, the structuring of the workstation facilities also affects its success. Therefore, management should insist that the technical people develop the types of tools and facilities that managers truly need to do their work. Only the managers know what they really need, so they must plan an important role in instructing the technicians, who are not managers, in specifically what is needed.

The lesson that this action offers is that you as a manager must be personally involved in the development and installation of workstation technology if it is to work. Unless managers recognize their role and execute that role, the workstations delivered to their offices will not perform the type of functions that they could have.

Managers are continually pulled in different directions in deciding how to allocate their time. Becoming involved with this new technology is another proposal demanding some of your time. However, the workstation is too important a concept to leave exclusively to the technicians.

WORKSTATION RULE OF THUMB

A proven principle of life states that you get out of any project what you put into it. If a manager puts none of himself into his workstation, he deserves what he gets.

DESIGNING AND IMPLEMENTING YOUR WORKSTATION

The workstation must be viewed as your staff. In fact, it is a fairly large staff and, properly managed, can do a lot of work. If you fail to train and direct your staff, you will be spending a lot of unnecessary time supervising. You must not forget that you are a manager when you begin using a workstation.

If the workstation is viewed as a subordinate, or staff of subordinates, then it should be subject to the same type of managerial controls as you apply to your staff of people. Whenever a manager fails to act as a manager, problems occur. The same skills that enabled you to be promoted to a manager must be used in managing your workstation. You must use these skills to help design, implement, and operate your workstation.

The managerial implementation strategies that are effective in addressing workstation technology are a basic set of managerial skills. These are listed in Fig. 3-1 and described below:

1: Set Objectives. Technicians stress the need for setting objectives during the experimentation phase of new technology. Managers know that unless objectives are set, little is accomplished. Management-by-objectives is a proven managerial strategy, and workstation technology should not be an exception to that rule.

Establish your own workstation objectives. The early objectives might relate to mastering workstation skills, building predetermined databases and files, or producing certain types of information using the workstation. The later goals should be much more specific and productivity-oriented. They should address both improved personal productivity and improved quality of work. For example, your goal could be a better analysis of the results produced by your people, or more timely information on delinquent accounts. Document your objective.

2: Develop a Workstation Work Plan. The objectives established for each workstation must be converted into a plan. The plan should determine how each objective will be accomplished. For example, to analyze delinquent accounts you will need a receivables database and a spreadsheet package, to spread receivables by age of account. The plan should indicate all the steps, including training, acquisition of software if needed, and so forth. Then, a schedule of events should be prepared.

Without establishing objectives and a plan to accomplish those objectives, the probability of success of a workstation is diminished. The reason over 20 percent of personal workstations are abandoned is because the user does not feel that worthwhile functions are being accomplished.

3: Establish a Workstation Budget. The resources allocated to the workstation should be budgeted. Some gauge is needed to determine how you are doing. As you maintain records on workstation use, your ability to budget will improve. The budget does not have to be formal; it can be maintained on a pad of paper.

The objective of maintaining records on workstation use is to monitor and improve workstation performance. The more detailed the performance information, the greater the opportunity for improvement. Determine those activities or events which you wish to control, for example, the time to load data into a database for processing, and then budget and measure those activities.

Number	Strategy	Description of Strategy
1.	Setting objectives	The goals to be accomplished through workstation processing should be identified and documented.
2.	Planning	A work program needs to be established to ensure that the goals will be accomplished.
3.	Budgeting	Funds must be allocated for workstation development and implementation, and then the use of those funds monitored.
4.	Organizing	The workstation activities must be organized in a manner such that there is adequate division of responsibilities, work is conducted in the appropriate priority, and the needed authority is incorporated into the work.
5.	Controlling	Adequate controls must be developed and installed to ensure the integrity and security of workstation processing.
6.	Evaluating	Feedback mechanisms must be developed to produce the information needed to monitor workstation performance and to ensure that the stated objectives are accomplished.

Fig. 3-1. Managerial implementation strategies.

At a minimum, it would be valuable to maintain records on both the cost of operating the workstation and the human resources consumed by it. This will enable you to estimate the cost-effectiveness of workstation processing. Although your company might not require this, it will help determine if you are doing the right tasks on the workstation. You can also compare these costs against your baseline.

The precision of these estimates does not have to be high. What the estimates should be showing are the magnitudes of difference between costs and benefits. For example, if you can do a task on a workstation for $100, and the benefits are $5,000, the precision of those estimates could be off significantly and still show the significant benefit of a workstation. For example, if it actually cost you $500 and the benefits were $2,500, the value of the workstation would be as apparent as if the initial precision was correct. The converse, where high costs provide low benefits, would also lead to the right decision regarding not performing that task on the workstation.

4: Organize Workstation Functions. Workstations are processing units with multiple capabilities. These capabilities can be provided individually, or they can be organized into cohesive support functions. For example, VisiCalc began as a single-purpose software package. It was not organized into a system of capabilities designed to assist the user to perform specific functions. The introduction of Lotus 1-2-3 offered multiple functions, including spreadsheets, graphics, and writing, into a single package, and became the leading software package overnight.

You should demand that the software and hardware provided for the workstation be organized to support your business tasks, not organized to make the workstation technically proficient. Individual managers might now know how to structure workstation capabilities, but you should immediately recognize which functions are difficult to perform and have them changed to make your processing easier.

5: Control the Workstation Activities. The controls needed by the workstation are a combination of automatic controls included in the workstation facilities and manual controls added by you. Ask, for each function performed on the workstation, "How do I know that the results will be correct?" Controls are the means of answering that question. For example, if you are protecting sales you must ask, "How do I know my projection is correct?" If you are dissatisfied with the answer to that question, or for any function, then additional controls should be added before you rely upon the results of that calculation.

6: Evaluate the Workstation Effectiveness. Previously it was stated that about 20 percent of the workstation users abandon the facility. For some reason the workstation was not serving a useful function for these users. If an evaluation is made and a problem can be identified, its cause might be eliminated so the workstation could be retained and eventually turned into a very effective managerial tool.

It is unrealistic to expect the initial workstation capabilities to be the optimum set of capabilities. The methods for doing work at the workstation need to be improved, adjusted, and extended. This is best done when measures are established regarding performance and productivity associated with workstation activities. For example, if your analysis of work indicates that you are spending too much time entering data into your workstation, you might look for alternate means of getting that data, such as obtaining it from the central computer site. Areas in which goals have not been met are the areas that need to be modified to improve performance.

WORKSTATION RULE OF THUMB
What you cannot measure, you cannot control. One of the key management workstation strategies should be to establish objectives and then measure to determine whether they have been achieved.

TURNING YOUR STRATEGIES INTO REALITIES

The strategies described in this chapter are designed to put you in charge of the workstation. The workstation is a tool provided to you to help perform your job function. Knowing what you want is not enough; understanding your role and strategies is not enough. You must make your plans happen.

The following four-step process is designed to put you in charge of the workstation process by using the previously described management strategies.

Number	Step	Description	Responsibilities
1.	Establish the workstation critical success factors	Defines the objectives (i.e., critical success factors) to be met through the use of a workstation	○ Senior management ○ Workstation user
2.	Assign workstation responsibility.	Identifies all of the tasks to be accomplished and ensure a single individual is responsible for each task	○ Workstation oversight group ○ Workstation user
3.	Install means to measure workstation performance.	Identifies areas to measure and then builds the method to collect and analyze the measurement data	○ Workstation oversight group ○ Workstation user
4.	Monitor and adjust workstation performance.	Using the feedback measurement data as a base, determines if objectives are being met, and if not, makes the necessary adjustment (to either or both objectives and workstation processes)	○ Workstation oversight group ○ Workstation user

Fig. 3-2. Implementing management strategies.

(See Fig. 3-2 for an overview of the implementation method.)

1: Establish the Workstation Critical Success Factors. You must determine what must be accomplished in order for the workstation to be successful. These are the objectives for installing the workstation. They should be expressed in terms of measurable factors. Some organizations call these critical success factors (CSF). For example, a CSF might be to create and have a memo in your staff's hands within one hour.

The tendency of managers using workstations is to experiment and use the workstation, and then judge whether or not it has been successful. Although this concept is frequently used, it is fraught with danger. The major danger is the lack of direction that occurs in this approach. It also leads to the high abandonment rate of the workstation.

The critical success factors do not need to be etched in concrete. The factors can change over time, but they provide direction and the basis for measurement of progress. It is important that the factors be stated in sufficient detail so that a decision can be made as to whether CSF has been accomplished.

Managers should resist the installation of the workstation until some specific objectives have been established. Once this is done, the workstation project becomes more believable and important to the manager. Without clear-cut objectives, it is often viewed as a toy.

The critical success factors do not have to be formally documented and distributed to anyone. They are for your use. Few organizations require the immediate justification of a managerial workstation. It is usually installed for one or two specific objectives, such as electronic mail, and then left to the manager to decide other uses. On the other hand, the determination of critical success factors has proved helpful to both the developers and installers of the workstation. It also increases the personal obligation of the manager to use the workstation for its intended purpose. Ownership is a powerful motivator of use.

2: Assign Workstation Responsibilities. Assigning responsibility for the performance of a task is important to ensure that a task is done. Unless a single individual is accountable and responsible for a task, it is a group effort, and frequently the group does not perform the desired task. Each member of the group waits for another member to take initiative.

It might appear that all components of the managerial workstation are the responsibility of the manager. This is not true. For example, maintenance of the hardware and software would certainly not be the manager's responsibility.

The workstation functions for which various individuals (technicians, managers, clerical staff members) should be responsible include:

- Selection of the workstation equipment.
- Installation of the workstation.
- Ordering workstation supplies.
- Hardware maintenance (both schedules and repair maintenance).

- Software maintenance (both preventive and repair maintenance).
- Initiating requests to modify workstation resources.
- Operating the workstation.
- Testing the proper functioning of workstation hardware and software.
- Developing workstation controls.
- Verifying the integrity of workstation-produced output.
- Ensuring adequate data backup for workstations.
- Developing workstation recovery procedures.
- Training workstation users.
- Ensuring the security of information processed by the workstation.
- Developing protocols and interfaces with other workstations and computers.

Each of these responsibilities needs to be assigned during the development and installation of the workstation. However, you as the user of the workstation might not be aware of who is responsible for some of these tasks, for example, maintenance of software. Questions then arise when a problem occurs—who should be called, and who will be responsible for fixing the problem, or enhancing the resources?

You should ask who is responsible for each of these tasks. Good management practices ensure that these responsibilities are properly assigned. The managerial strategies of organizing and planning deal with assignment of responsibilities. Organizing is the assignment of the responsibility, and planning is ensuring that the responsibility can be fulfilled.

3: Install Means to Measure Workstation Performance. What you cannot measure, you cannot control. Unless you can establish measures, and then collect that information, you will have great difficulty in controlling workstation performance. For example, if you do not know how much time you spend performing certain tasks, such as composing a letter, you might do tasks on a workstation which could be more economically performed by other means, such as dictating to a secretary. Also, certain types of problems might occur repetitively, but without record, the frequency will not be known. Thus, action that should be taken will not be taken.

Measurement is a two-edged sword. Whatever is measured tends to be controlled. If the wrong item is measured, the wrong variable will be controlled. For example, if the time needed to produce a sales project is the important area to measure, but the analysis is just produced on time, it will be worthless.

The measures can be established by both the central group overseeing the workstation, as well as by you. It is not important who establishes the measures, as long as good measures are established. Normally, the data processing people will establish technical measures such as up-time, while you should establish business measures such as timeliness of results.

The type of items that might be measured include:

- Dollars expended on workstations.

- Hours expended by users.
- Hours expended by the support group.
- Number and frequency of workstation application uses.
- Hours of workstation use per day.
- Types and frequencies of problems encountered.
- Hours of training.
- Reduction in hours to perform tasks.
- Increases in productivity.
- Resources provided to managers, but not used.
- Increases or decreases in the amount of use of identified resources.
- Types and frequencies of requests for additional resources.

Wherever possible, the measurement information should be collected automatically. For example, costs might be collected through a budgeting system, and work hours through a time-reporting system. If support assistance is needed, the people providing support, such as hardware maintenance, can report their time independently.

Reporting of information to measure performance should not cost more than the benefit derived from collecting that information. The information collected should be available to the individual managers, as well as to the central group overseeing the operation of workstations for the organization.

4: Monitor and Adjust Workstation Performance. One of the major functions of the group that develops and installs the workstation is to provide the necessary oversight and direction to accomplish stated objectives. If realistic objectives has been established and the feedback mechanisms indicate they are being accomplished, adjustments are not necessary. On the other hand, if the feedback data indicates that the objectives are not being accomplished, managerial action needs to be taken. For example, if there is too much down time due to faulty hardware, it might need to be replaced. This is the primary objective for measuring performance. The earlier these adjustments can be made, the greater the benefit to you by not having to live with poor performance.

If your objectives are not being met, you have two options (both can be selected). First, the processes which are used by the workstation can be adjusted. For example, more training, different software, or different operating procedures might be required. Second, the objectives can be changed. It might be that the objectives are unrealistic, inappropriate, and should be changed. As objectives are changed, the feedback mechanisms that measure the performance of those objectives might also have to be changed.

WORKSTATION RULE OF THUMB
Managers using managerial processes remain in charge of technology. You can rarely control technology using technical strategies.

32

IMPEDIMENTS AND COUNTERSTRATEGIES
TO TAKING CHARGE OF WORKSTATION IMPLEMENTATION

Knowing what to do and doing it are two separate issues. You might recognize that you need to be in charge, but have difficulty establishing the direction implementation is taking. This is particularly true in a highly technical area such as software selection. The central group might decide that they know what you need better than you do.

The objective of this section is to indicate why the action might be difficult to accomplish. Counterstrategies are given for each of the identified impediments.

Impediment 1: Caught Up in the Technology. Technology has its own jargon and its own mystique. As people become involved in technology, they frequently become consumed by the technological processes. For example, the manager using the workstation wants to master the technical jargon and the workstation processes, instead of managing the business process. In other words, you become a technician instead of acting as a manager.

The counterstrategy is to establish a managerial approach before using the technology. If your management approaches, such as planning, are fully defined before you accept technology, the managerial role cannot be overlooked. On the other hand, if you attempt to master technology prior to establishing the managerial controls, those controls might never be established.

Impediment 2: Central Ownership of Your Workstation. Many managers wonder who owns the workstation. Frequently, the technicians look at the workstations as theirs, because they ordered and set it up, rather than as yours. Whoever owns the workstation becomes responsible for the proper functioning of it, and as long as "they" are responsible, you are not.

The counterstrategy is to make yourself responsible for the workstation. Methods must be used to ensure that the user of the workstation is the individual responsible for the workstation. When you accept ownership and responsibility, you will begin applying managerial processes to ensure the proper functioning of the workstation.

SELF-ASSESSMENT CHECKLIST

Assessment is another managerial process. Therefore, it is logical to assess whether or not this implementation action has been appropriately managed. The objective of this part of the chapter is to provide a tool for that self-assessment.

A self-assessment checklist for this chapter's action is provided as Fig. 3-3. The checklist contains a list of items that assess your accomplishment of the materials presented in this chapter. It is structured so that "yes" responses indicate effective actions, while "no" responses might represent potential problems or impediments to the successful use of the workstation. A comments column is provided to explain "no" responses. These should be

Item	Response			
	Yes	No	N/A	Comments
1. Have the duties/tasks being performed by the manager been identified?				
2. Has a profile of usage for the managers's work been developed?				
3. Has the workstation been customized for the manager's work?				
4. Has the manager participated in this workstation customization?				
5. Does the manager accept the fact that he or she must manage the workstation as a subordinate?				
6. Does the manager accept responsibility for the performance of work performed by the workstation?				
7. Have objectives been established for workstation performance?				
8. Have these objectives been stated in measurable terms (e.g., critical success factors)?				
9. Has the manager developed a work plan for accomplishing the workstation objectives?				
10. Has a budget been established for workstation acquisition and operation?				
11. Have the tasks to be accomplished on the workstation been identified?				
12. Has a single individual been assigned responsibility for each workstation task, so that person can be held accountable for that task?				
13. Have feedback mechanisms been established to measure the execution of each critical factor?				
14. Are the feedback mechanisms in place and working?				
15. Does the manager get reports on that feedback information and are the objectives, and workstation methods adjusted accordingly?				
16. Has the workstation manager identified areas requiring control, and established control for those areas?				

Fig. 3-3. The management strategies self-assessment checklist.

investigated to determine whether action should be taken to address the issue. The results of that investigation should also be recorded in the comments column. These self-assessments should be made periodically, because as conditions change, new problems surface. If they are not addressed, they might lower workstation performance.

WORKSTATION RULE OF THUMB
If you know where you want to go, and then periodically check the roadmap to ensure you are going in the right direction, you usually get there. The self-assessment process is that assurance checking.

Chapter 4

Action 2: Become
Workstation Friendly

*The time spent learning the machine before you use it will be
returned many times because you can do the job right the first time.*

This chapter explains how to use the experimentation phase effectively on the
workstation. During this period, you are free to experiment, make errors, and
solve problems without the threat of having to rely on the workstation-produced
results. The process is one of learning the workstation, the application capabilities, and the analysis routines included with the workstation. This chapter
lays out a plan for mastering the basic workstation skills, at the same time
ensuring that the workstation is customized to your specific needs.

Learning to operate a workstation is similar to learning how to drive a car.
The basic operations are simple, but when you get in trouble there is no substitute for experience. With an hour or two of instruction, an individual can
begin driving an automobile, but it might take several years to become an accomplished driver.

Let's look at two typical problems that might confront the new driver. First,
an unusual noise might come from the engine which is difficult to interpret.
Second, the driver might experience some abnormal handling conditions, which
might seem normal to the new driver, who does not have a basis for comparison. Also, reaction to emergency situations has not been practiced so the wrong
action, or no action, might occur. These same problems and frustrations occur to new workstation users.

GIVE ME ONE DAY OF YOUR TIME AND I WILL WORK A MIRACLE

Managers are busy people. There is rarely time in a day to do activities other than the ones required by the job. Time to think is often a luxury. On the other hand, you cannot afford to go without training because the mistakes made will eat up too much of your valuable time. Spare one day and your return on investment will be huge. Reasons for not experimenting with the workstation include:

- Lack of available time.
- Available time does not coincide with formal training sessions.
- Subordinates can perform many of the basic functions (particularly essential ones).
- Working at a keyboard is not perceived as a managerial function.
- Manager lacks minimal data processing skills needed as a prerequisite to learning a workstation.

The consequences of nonexperimentation include:

- Ineffective use of the workstation.
- Abandonment of the workstation.
- Transferring workstation responsibility to a subordinate.
- Increased error rate.
- Inaccurate and/or incomplete workstation processing.
- Excessive calls for assistance.

A problem that affects training is a manager not wanting to look ignorant in front of subordinates. Two different forces are in effect, making it difficult for some managers to accept training. The first is that training might come from subordinates. This means that the manager will not be in a dominant position but, rather, becomes dependent upon the subordinate(s). The second concern is one of showing ignorance about the wonderful world of data processing. The manager might have been around computers for many years but has gained minimal computer knowledge, which will become obvious to everyone when workstation instruction begins. The degree of seriousness of this concern varies from manager to manager.

The concept of sparing one day of your time for training is important. The one day is a learning experience, to acquire new capabilities. For example, one day might be devoted to learning electronic mail, one day to learning how to build and use directories, and one day for each major processing capability. In some instances, more time would be desirable, but one day devoted to any topic is enough to get started. That day does not have to be a contiguous eight-hour day but, rather, can be spread over many days, or involve some evenings.

If you expect to use any new technology and capability without training, you are kidding yourself. A famous commercial indicates "you can pay me now, or you can pay me later." As the ad implies, the up-front cost is significantly less than the pay-me-later cost. If you will invest that day into training at the start, the types and severity of problems that you will encounter later on will be minimal. That is the payback for the one day of training.

When you know how to interact with machine processing, you will feel comfortable doing it, as well as find it relatively easy to do. Knowledge in how to use a capability makes that capability seem "friendly" to you.

The action proposed in this chapter will not take much more than a day of your time. It does not require a full workday expended at once but, rather, an organized approach to learning the workstation, which requires two things: a mastery of the workstation basic capabilities and the availability of capabilities that meet your needs.

WORKSTATION TRAINING STRATEGIES

The period of workstation training can be one of pleasure or panic. Some managers enjoy learning a new skill and using advanced technology, but many managers panic about the prospects of entering the computer age. Pleasure is preferable over panic.

Scheduling and attitude are the countermeasures to panic. If you set aside adequate time for learning the workstation, you need not be concerned about your ability to perform on it. A positive mental attitude is helpful. Recognize that any skill can be mastered with sufficient time and effort.

WORKSTATION RULE OF THUMB
Franklin Delano Roosevelt could have had concepts like the workstation in mind when he said, "The only thing we have to fear is fear itself."

Strategies are the means by which a manager attacks challenges and problems. Selecting the appropriate strategy for mastering workstation technology will be partially dependent upon your personal data processing background and experience. The more experienced you are in using data processing equipment, the easier workstation mastery will become.

The five survival strategies that you can select from to help you master the complexity of computer workstations are summarized in Fig. 4-1 and described in the following sections.

1: Utilize Company Training Program (Preferred Strategy). Organizations in search of excellence devote a proportionally larger amount of effort for training than do less successful corporations. Although training alone will not make an excellent organization, the lack of training might detract from that excellence. Extensive training is also one of the principles used by Dr. W. Edwards Deming, the individual noted for the productivity turnaround in Japanese industry, making quality in Japanese products a reality.

Number	Strategy	Description
1.	Utilize company training program (preferred strategy).	Use the training facilities provided by the company to learn the workstation.
2.	Tough it out.	Learn the workstation by sitting at the workstation and using it.
3.	Take a data processing fundamentals course. (Most community colleges offer such a course.)	Prior to learning the workstation, master the fundamentals of data processing.
4.	Use a tutor (preferred strategy).	Engage the services of an expert to teach you individually.
5.	Do it yourself.	Learn during nonworking hours, normally on one's own equipment.

Fig. 4-1. Workstation mastery strategies.

Company workstation programs should include training programs. In some organizations, these are formal classroom sessions, while others use self-study manuals. In addition, the training is frequently embedded into the workstation software as "help" routines. These routines provide direction for users when called. In many systems, the user can type the word "HELP" on the keyboard to invoke routines which show how to perform the task correctly.

Rarely will a single form of training suffice to convert the unskilled user into a fully productive workstation user. The value of company training will be partially dependent upon the variety of training experiences provided. At a minimum, these training experiences should include the following:

• A workstation concepts program, which provides an explanation of the purposes, benefits, and objectives for managers using workstation processing, as well as the capabilities and limitations of workstations. This is normally short in duration, for example, one to two hours.

• Classroom training, providing an opportunity for potential users to receive formal instruction on how the workstation functions. These sessions might run from one day to one week. The sessions normally provide classroom instruction coupled with case studies, exercises, and hands-on experience.

• On-site, one-on-one training, designed to supplement other types of training. Working one-on-one with the user helps solve specific operational problems. It should occur while the formal training sessions are taking place, as well as when people encounter problems in operating the workstation.

• Workstation manuals should be provided. At a minimum, this would include the operations manual for the workstation equipment and manuals for using application software. The clarity and ease of use of the manuals is a factor in determining the amount of classroom and one-on-one instruction that needs to be provided.

• Help routines included within the workstation capabilities to lead the user through difficult-to-perform functions, or to help when the user gets into trouble. For example, if you are unsure what command to enter to complete a task, the help routine would explain to you the options available and/or suggest a command.

• A help desk (actually a telephone number) provided workstation users to obtain assistance. It is a lower-priced alternative to the one-on-one, on-site instruction.

2: Tough It Out (Not a Recommended Strategy). This strategy is for the individual who doesn't believe in taking the time for formal training. This is usually a person with computer knowledge who is willing to sit down at the workstation and begin processing—the same type of person who attempts to put a do-it-yourself product together without reading the instructions.

The tough-it-out user tends to bypass the experimentation phase and move right to production. This individual wants to get productive work on-line as quickly as possible. Formal courses and other time-consuming activity slow down the pace at which this individual likes to work. The tough-it-out concept is also used because courses might be inconveniently scheduled for a manager. For example, the courses might be every Friday at nine in the morning, and that individual has a competing staff meeting or other commitment for that time.

The tough-it-out concept works best if the individual is skilled in data processing concepts and principles. However, the tough-it-out user frequently needs a workstation consultant and help routines if they are available. A user knowledgeable in interactive processing routines can become productive quickly with the aid of good help routines.

3: Take a Data Processing Fundamentals Course (Strongly Recommended for People Who Do Not Understand Data Processing Principles). This strategy could be called "back to the basics." The approach is one of learning the basic data processing principles prior to using the workstation. For example, understanding concepts such as data structures (e.g., records and files) might prove to be very helpful in mastering the workstation.

In mastering any new skill, terminology is always a problem. There might be implications and principles behind words that are not readily apparent. This leads people to overreact to minor situations, and underestimate to the more serious ones. A solid foundation in data processing fundamentals can help put the workstation's operations into the proper perspective.

Courses in computer fundamentals are available through community colleges, books, video cassettes, special conferences, and seminars.

4: Hire a Tutor (Recommended Strategy for Busy Managers). Many managers are reluctant to be instructed by subordinates, or do not have time to go back and forth to classes. As previously discussed, there can be business conflicts regarding times of prescheduled courses.

One alternative to formal classroom study is to engage a special tutor. This might be someone provided by the organization, or it might be an outside consultant. Many executives already use tutors to learn foreign languages or other special skills. Although a tutor is always more costly than a formal classroom situation, tutoring might prove to be significantly quicker because the tutor can customize and address specific problems. A tutor can avoid the generalities that occur in a classroom situation.

When a tutor is used, the student should set some specific educational objectives. The tutor should be familiar with the workstation capabilities, and approximately how this particular workstation will be used. It is this customization that makes tutoring work.

5: Do It Yourself. Some believe that if you want things to be done right, you have to do them yourself. In mastering workstation skills, this means learning about the workstation during nonworking hours. In most instances, it involves learning at home using a microcomputer to practice or simulate workstation skills.

There are three primary reasons why an individual would want to attempt to master workstation skills at home. First, there might be a lack of time. The manager might prefer some of the other strategies, but not have adequate time available during the day. Although any manager can free up some time, large blocks of uninterrupted time might be difficult to obtain. For example, if, while working on the workstation, there is a constant stream of telephone calls and interruptions, the manager would not get the opportunity to devote the amount of attention needed to master a new skill. Some managers do not have the opportunity to turn off the workday by closing their office door.

Second, there might be an unavailability to meet scheduled training classes. A manager might be able to find time, but not when it is consistent with the schedule provided for formal training. Thus, a scheduling conflict might cause the manager to seek other paths for learning workstation skills.

Finally, a manager might prefer not to learn on the job. There are a variety of reasons why individuals would not want to learn the workstation skill on the job. These vary from the incorrect concept of "you can't teach an old dog new tricks" to the normal emotion of not wanting to look stupid in front of one's peers and subordinates.

Fortunately, old dogs can learn new tricks. It might take longer, but if the desire is there, the skills are masterable. Some companies offer incentives to managers to use workstations. One organization provided workstations at no cost to a department budget if the manager of that department would use one, but if the manager didn't use one the cost of all workstations used in the department would be included within the manager's budget.

If an individual can master a personal computer, that individual can master a workstation. The concepts are basically the same. Therefore, managers concerned about on-the-job time associated with learning can acquire a relatively low-cost personal computer and master the same or similar software programs at home on their own equipment. For example, if the office workstation includes a spreadsheet package, the concepts of using a spreadsheet package can be learned on a personal computer at home, even though it is not the same vendor package used at work. It would be like learning to drive in one car, and then being given another car by your business to drive.

LEARNING THE WORKSTATION IN ONE DAY

A four-step program is provided to assist you in learning the workstation. The first step asks you to learn basic computer concepts. This should be done prior to your one day on-the-job training program. The remaining three steps are on-the-job steps which will lead you through mastering sufficient skills to permit you to begin using the workstation. Use a full day to experiment and learn, and not only will your confidence go up, but your error level should drop significantly as you begin to work using this new capability.

You must accept the responsibility for learning the workstation. Although others can assist in this responsibility, they cannot substitute for going through the learning cycle. The workstation is designed to be an aid and extension of your personal capabilities. Therefore, the use of the workstation should not be transferred to a subordinate.

Learning can be made easy or difficult by the method and sequence in which the skills are taught. Unfortunately, the training programs for workstations are frequently put together by technicians, rather than educators. Some probing questions by you about the training materials should prove helpful in evaluating the potential effectiveness of training materials.

A four-step process for mastering workstation skills is listed in Fig. 4-2 and described below.

1: Learn Computer Concepts. Some people might argue that it is not necessary to understand how a car works to drive one. This argument appears reasonable until the automobile fails to function properly. It is at that point where a basic knowledge of the automobile pays off. Neither the basic knowledge about an automobile nor data processing is difficult to master.

There are two basic concepts of computer processing that are valuable to understand. The first is about data and the second deals with how that data is processed.

Data is divided into four categories. The data element is the smallest piece of intelligible data, for example, an employee number or product quantity. The data element is sometimes called a data item or a field.

The record is a group of data elements held together by a common bond. The bond is usually a relationship to a certain type of processing. In manual systems, a record would be a document. The bond that holds information together on a document is usually the description of a document such as a purchase order, timecard, or shipping notice. Sometimes records are subdivisions of paper documents, for example, a purchase order might be a document, but

Number	Step	Description	Responsibilities
1.	Learn computer concepts.	Understand the data hierarchy and processing concept (use fundamentals course, company training program, or tutor strategies).	° Workstation user
2.	Learn the workstation keyboard and functions.	Determine how to run jobs as a workstation operator (use company training course, tutor, tough-it-out, or do-it-yourself strategies).	° Workstation user
3.	Learn the workstation capabilities (i.e., all of the job aids included with the workstation).	Identify the tasks included with the workstation and what they are designed to accomplish (use company training course or do-it-yourself strategies).	° Workstation user
4.	Experiment with the usable applications.	Learn how the needed workstation applications work (use company training course, tutor, tough-it-out, or do-it-yourself strategies).	° Workstation user

Fig. 4-2. Methods to master workstation skills.

a single line item on the purchase order might be a record, and the ordering information such as where to ship and who to bill could be another record.

The file is a group of records held together by a common bond. For example, all of the payroll records would be a payroll file, and all of the purchase orders would be an order entry file.

The database is a collection of several files in a single repository of data. This grouping of data is normally managed by a database management system. The totality of data within the database is normally referred to as a *schema*, and the portion of the database used in a single operation is called a *subschema* (i.e., the equivalent of a stand-alone file).

Much of the work performed by the workstation user will be manipulating data. Thus, it is important to understand data, the attributes of each element of data, and the hierarchy of data within a workstation environment. The definition of a data element is very precise, and any variances from that precision will cause problems in processing. For example, if the definition of a data element that is used in computation is four positions in length, the entry of a five-position number in that four-position field would result in one position being lost.

One of the concepts you will quickly learn about any type of computer processing is that it is very detailed and precise. Each task must be performed in a certain sequence. You must follow the rules precisely. Each interactive question must be answered in the right way, or processing does not continue in the proper manner. You must accept this as a fact of life in computer-related processing, because the computer itself can only perform certain types of tasks, and the processing that you need to fulfill your job responsibilities must be completed using the capabilities of the computer.

Conceptually, a computer can only do one of the following three things at a time: Move data, perform arithmetic, or make a comparison.

Moving data involves reading, storing, displaying, printing it. The computer can perform mathematical computations, or make a comparison by determining whether one value is equal to, higher, or lower than another value. A comparison can include letters, numbers, and special characters such as dollar signs.

All computer processing is performed by using these three operations. Thus, even what might appear to be simple tasks might require you to use many different commands, and the computer program might perform thousands more. Understanding computer programming, and basic systems design, although not necessary, will help explain how computers work. Now begins your one-day-on-the-job training.

2: Learn the Workstation Keyboard and Functions. Frequently, one of the major deterrents to using the workstation is the inability of the user to master the keyboard. Workstation keyboards are arranged in the same basic format as typewriter keyboards. Unfortunately, if a manager has not mastered the typewriter keyboard, that challenge will carry over to workstation processing. While the "hunt and peck" system works, it can be slow and frustrating.

The workstation keyboard is normally supplemented by a set of command or function keys. They type and number of keyboard commands will vary from workstation to workstation. The objective of these command keys is to permit the workstation operator to interact with the workstation to perform certain actions, such as indicate which of two alternatives is wanted.

The more common command keys include:

- Load. This key starts processing so the operator can begin using the workstation.
- Escape. This permits the operator to leave the current task being performed and move to another task.
- Cursor keys. These move the position on the screen where data can be entered. The cursor is the flashing light on a video screen that indicates where data entered on the keyboard will be placed on the screen.
- Return. This command informs the workstation that a subtask has been completed and you want to begin another subtask; for example, you entered

a telephone number in a directory, and are now ready to enter another.

The function keys vary from workstation to workstation. The above names are common on many workstations, but are not universally used. Therefore, the type of action indicated might be associated with a function or command key known by a different name.

The function keys are closely associated with the *operating system* provided by the workstation. An operating system is an internal manager which directs the work of the computer. The operating system (i.e., the internal manager) communicates what task the manager wants to perform. Operating systems contain a group of commands for the user. These are frequently displayed on the screen in the form of a *menu*, which is a listing of actions or routines that are available to the user. These commands include capabilities such as duplicating files, listing files, and selecting workstation tasks.

You can learn the keyboard and workstation functions in one of two ways. You can either read the manuals and follow the instructions, or you can have someone walk you through the basic commands. Do not try to learn all the commands the first day. Learn only enough to be able to use the workstation, for example, to build and use a telephone directory, or to communicate with others in an electronic mail system. Even after some classroom instruction, you will need time to practice these skills.

At the end of this step, you will understand how to get programs in and out of computer memory, how to load computer files, how to operate the keyboard, and how to perform the maintenance necessary on a workstation, such as duplicating files. Understanding computer concepts will help explain the need for learning and using these keyboard operations and functions. At this point, you are ready to begin some useful work on the workstation.

3: Learn the Workstation Capabilities. As a workstation user, you will be provided with an inventory of job-related applications. As discussed earlier in this book, these applications, such as word processing, should be customized for your responsibilities. Normally, the inventory of capabilities will contain more capabilities than you will use, at least initially. It should, however, contain all of the capabilities you really need to be using the workstation.

You should become familiar with applications important to you which are contained in the inventory provided on your workstation. These applications should be described on workstation menus. This menu is how you select the specific application you want. Normally the menu description is very cryptic, but descriptions included in user manuals should be easy to read and understand.

The emphasis of this step is to learn "how" the applications work. This step does not involve using the application to process data but, rather, identifying and understanding the types of capabilities available to the user. There are three tasks involved in performing this step:

44

- Obtain or create a list of applications included with your workstation.
- Identify the applications of interest; limit this to the two or three most important applications for you.
- Learn the capabilities of the more important applications.

These tasks are not difficult if you approach them from a logical perspective. The first thing that you want to learn is what types of reports or outputs are produced by the application. What you are trying to find out is what the application can do for you. For example, a telephone directory program will provide you with the telephone number of someone included in the directory; it might also dial that number for you.

You have to determine what you need to do in order to make a capability happen. For the example of the telephone directory, you might be able to get a telephone number by entering a person's name, or by using a special code word. For example, if you wanted my telephone number you might be able to type in William E. Perry, or you might be able to get it if you had a prearranged system of code, such as typing "Bill." If, in addition to typing that, you pushed a special command or function key, for example, function key one (designated on the keyboard key as "F1"), the system would also dial that number for you.

You must understand what type of data to enter into the computer in order for a process to work. Again, with the example of the directory, you would have to enter the telephone number, the name of the person, and all of the codes that you might want to enter to identify that telephone number. Previously I said that if you typed in the code word "Bill" you would get my telephone number. When you do this, you must use a unique code or codes for each telephone number.

The example of the directory is a simple processing capability. If the capability that you had was to control inventory or calculate economic order quantities for inventory, the effort would be more complex. However, you would still follow the same sequence of events to learn the application.

4: Experiment with the Needed Application. This final step involves learning to use the applications of interest (i.e., those identified in Step 3). The three previous steps have been preparatory for this one. This is the most important step, but probably cannot be performed until the previous three steps have been mastered.

Experimentation with applications involves entering test transactions to determine how processing works. Some applications contain a capability to experiment. For example, a word processing package might contain a sample letter that you can use to learn how to modify a letter. If no such test capability is provided with the application, the user will have to create small files and then process against them. The types of experimenting that should be tried are those tasks that you will be using for business purposes.

The best way to learn an application is to actually use it. In the telephone directory example, the best way to learn would be to enter a few telephone numbers in the directory, use the directory to call up those telephone numbers, and actually initiate telephone calls. Most applications have a method for eliminating unwanted data, so if you used your application in a learning mode, you might have to delete the practice data before you began using the application for business purposes.

The user will already have identified the types of processing capabilities desired, and the types of outputs wanted. It is these tasks and reports that the user should experiment processing and producing.

At the end of these four steps, you will not have completely mastered your workstation. You will, however, have mastered the fundamentals of workstation operation, and have a general knowledge of how to use the two or three applications most important to you. You are now ready for real work on the workstation, which will continue to improve your skills through practice. These four steps need not take longer than a day, but without them the time to produce accurate and complete processing might seem endless.

WORKSTATION RULE OF THUMB
It is always better to spend time learning to do it right the first time than to expend time redoing it.

The training strategies that are helpful in accomplishing these steps have been listed in the description column of Fig. 4-2. For each step there are several strategies that can be used. The manager should use that strategy which feels most comfortable. This is the "old shoe" approach, but it usually produces the best results.

IMPEDIMENTS AND COUNTERSTRATEGIES TO BECOMING WORKSTATION FRIENDLY

There is no substitute for practice in mastering workstation skills. There is value to textbook and classroom training, but mastery requires use of the workstation. The steps described in this chapter represent a workable approach to learning. However, in practice, nothing is easy.

There are three impediments that inhibit many managers from mastering computer technology.

Impediment 1: The Management Ego. Some managers feel uncomfortable admitting they don't understand something like the computer. President Abdel Nasser of Egypt once said that it was the leader's job to find which way the mob was going, and then get out front and lead it. Although the mob is using workstations, many leaders are reluctant to get out in front of the mob and lead it through effective workstation usage.

The counterstrategy is to provide a workstation for home usage, to create a learning environment that does not embarrass the learner. This might mean providing a manager with a workstation to take home for learning and experimenting, or providing for making mistakes in private. You want to ensure the manager will be successful in using the system with the subordinates or work colleagues involved.

Impediment 2: The Old Way Works. Many managers are reluctant to try a new way when they know the existing way works. These managers have had success using existing technology, but are uncertain about whether they will achieve that same level of success using a new way. It becomes a matter of giving up a workable way for something that might not work as well.

The counterstrategy is based on the principle that success breeds confidence. In introducing a new technology it is best to go slowly so that users of that technology experience initial success. When the manager masters the basic uses of a workstation, the manager will be encouraged to use more advanced procedures, which, if successful, will encourage still more usage.

Impediment 3: Inability to Manage Time. Peter Drucker, a noted management consultant, states that many managers lose control of their workday. Telephone calls, interruptions, and meetings rob them of the ability to schedule their work in such a manner that it can be performed during the workday. Time management is too big a problem to address head-on with workstations, but the negative impact of time management needs to be assessed if it affects managers mastering workstation skills.

The counterstrategy involves off-premises experimentation. Two counterstrategies can be used to overcome time management problems. The first is a "fat farm" technique. This involves physically removing the manager from the existing work environment, and moving that manager to another environment. This is the concept used when people need to lose weight but cannot do it in their own environment; they must be moved to an environment in which their caloric intake can be controlled. In workstation training, this translates to taking the training in a location other than the office.

The second counterstrategy is to provide nonwork opportunities to master workstations. This can be done immediately preceding the workday, following the workday, on Saturdays, or at the individual's home. The time that appears best for the manager should be worked out, and the educational opportunities made available which best fit into the manager's schedule.

SELF-ASSESSMENT CHECKLIST

Mastering workstation skills involves both the teaching process and the individual's attitude. This self-assessment checklist is designed to evaluate the teaching process. A good workstation educational curriculum, however, will not ensure the success of the workstation program. An environment must exist in the company which encourages the use of workstations by those who

Item	Response			
	Yes	No	N/A	Comments
1. Have the educational objectives for workstation operation been established?				
2. Have the individuals requiring education been identified?				
3. Has someone been appointed to be accountable and responsible for developing the educational material?				
4. Has a method been developed to advise potential candidates of the availability of educational offerings?				
5. Do educational offerings include stand-up classroom education?				
6. Do educational offerings include self-study/procedural manuals?				
7. Do educational offerings include help routines built into the workstation processing?				
8. Do educational offerings include on-site counseling, if needed?				
9. Does the educational process include a method to evaluate mastery of workstation skills?				
10. As new workstation procedures/methods are developed, will there be educational offerings associated with those improvements?				
11. Have the educational offerings been designed to meet the scheduling and time commitments of managers?				
12. Are off-site (e.g., home) educational opportunities offered for the manager who has neither time nor inclination to acquire those skills during normal working hours?				
13. Has an educational curriculum been offered that outlines the steps and courses recommended to master workstation skills?				
14. Do the students taking the educational offerings have an opportunity to evaluate the effectiveness of those offerings?				
15. Have the managerial candidates been provided an opportunity to indicate the type of courses they would like to have to assist them in mastering workstation technology?				

Fig. 4-3. The workstation mastery self-assessment checklist.

want to use the new technology.

A self-assessment checklist for evaluating the workstation educational curriculum is provided as Fig. 4-3. The checklist is based on the materials presented in this chapter. "Yes" responses to the checklist indicate good educational practices, while "no" responses might indicate that additional educational offerings or methods should be incorporated into the curriculum.

WORKSTATION RULE OF THUMB

The Japanese concept of "right in time" must be applied to managerial training for workstations. The training must be available at the time needed by the manager.

Chapter 5

Action 3: Use the Workstation Effectively

The workstation should support you in the same manner that your staff supports you. The objective of the workstation is to simplify your tasks so that you can concentrate your effort on the most important tasks.

This chapter describes how to ensure that the workstation will fit into your way of doing work. A step-by-step procedure is provided to build a matrix which shows how the workstation will support your job tasks. The matrix is prepared to help you develop new day-to-day job procedures. The chapter includes a self-assessment checklist to help you ensure that the workstation will assist you in fulfilling your job responsibilities effectively.

Your workstation should be a productivity tool. Two types of productivity should be increased. First, you should need fewer staff members because staff functions can be automated and processed on the workstation. Second, your personal productivity should be improved through the use of more effective support routines aiding in the performance of managerial functions.

THE NEED FOR PROCEDURES

One of the principles of productivity that is important to understand is that hard work might not improve productivity. Many managers believe that if people work harder, productivity will be increased. However, it is the effective use of tools that increases productivity.

Let's look at two farmers plowing their fields. The first farmer uses a horse-drawn plow. The second farmer has a modern farm tractor. The farmer with the horse-drawn plow ends the day exhausted, and will only plow a small amount of land. The farmer using the tractor can plow many times as much land as the other farmer, and finish the day less tired. The difference in productivity is the tool used by the farmers, not the amount of effort put into the job. On the other hand, the introduction of the tractor added other tasks which did not exist before, such as oil changes. This causes the farmer to perform different tasks.

The workstation is the new tool of the manager. If this tool is improperly used, it will not provide the hoped-for productivity gains. Having the right tool is a key element in increasing one's personal productivity, but equally important is the development of procedures to use that tool. These procedures are important to the success of the workstation because they enable you to do the following:

- Define the needed work steps.
- Reconcile language to the terminology you and your staff use.
- Divide difficult tasks into simple steps.
- Integrate manual tasks with automated tasks.
- Provide a standardized method which can be improved.

The principle is to develop procedures explaining how the workstation is to be used in performing your work tasks. This action is neither time-consuming nor difficult. It is, however, one of the ingredients for workstation effectiveness.

AREAS FOR WORKSTATION PROCEDURES

The four areas that you should consider developing to assist in selecting workstation procedures are listed in Fig. 5-1 and individually described below.

Area 1: Data Movement. Workstation users quickly become "data starved" unless procedures are established to ensure a steady flow of data. Centralized databases provide the main source of data for analytical purposes. Workstations can also become "data choked" unless they can *upload* their data to corporate facilities. Uploading means transmitting data from your workstation to a central computer facility.

Downloading of data, the process of acquiring data from central computer databases, will quickly be recognized as an important workstation need. The design of workstations frequently includes access to corporate data. However, data not included in the workstation package might be needed, or data provided might be in the wrong format.

In downloading data, the needed data is physically transferred from the central computer site to workstation disk storage. Once the data is physically transmitted to the workstation, you can perform unlimited analyses on that data. It is the same concept as providing a manager with a report, but with

Number	Strategy	Description
1.	Data movement	Ensure that data needed in other locations can be transferred to workstation for processing, and processed data can be transferred to other locations.
2.	Application operation	Ensure that all needed work tasks will be properly performed.
3.	Obtaining assistance	Locate reference materials and people who can provide insight and advice on what can be performed on a workstation.
4.	Sharing knowledge	Interact with other workstation users for the purposes of sharing solutions to current problems, and requesting changes or additions to current workstations capabilities.

Fig. 5-1. Areas needing workstation procedures.

a workstation there is the added capability to analyze that data using workstation capabilities.

Workstations can interact with data in a corporate database, but the process is different, and so are the capabilities. For example, the workstation user might want data of a previous date, but the data in the central database is current as of this moment. The workstation user might want data from several files of databases combined, which would prove to be an exceedingly difficult workstation task to perform. Also, the workstation user might need the data in a different format in order to analyze that data using workstation software. For example, certain spreadsheet packages require predetermined data formats.

Both downloading and uploading data require certain facilities. Normally, these involve transforming data into the format that is needed for processing. In addition, new security procedures might be needed to ensure the protection of data at the workstation site.

Data can be downloaded or uploaded in two ways. In the first, diskettes are physically transmitted. The needed data can be recorded on a diskette by either the central or remote site. The diskette is then physically carried to the other site where it is read and used. The second uses electronic transmission to transmit the needed data electronically over communication lines from one site to the other.

Area 2: Application Operation. Most workstation applications represent basic processing capabilities. For example, the spreadsheet software package is a matrix capability which you can use to spread costs or other data among predetermined entities, such as spreading the acquisitions made by major customers over the months in which they made those acquisitions. However, the spreadsheet package does not indicate how to use the matrix capability in the day-to-day functioning of your job.

Most workstation capabilities perform part of a needed task, but do not perform the entire task. For example, for the spreadsheet analysis, you will need to gather data before you can process it, and then might have to make some analysis and take action after you have completed the workstation processing. Therefore, the procedures which define how the spreadsheet works are not the same as the procedures that you need to perform the full task.

Developing procedures for workstation processing, like most of the other actions indicated in this book, is not a time-consuming task. The process is one of planning and preparation, as opposed to preparing very formal documents. Many managers use a pad of paper to document the procedures. Although the format does not have to be elaborate, it is very helpful to write out the procedures. Procedures can be written in longhand; they do not need to be typed, although you could use the workstation word processing capabilities to document the procedures.

An example of the procedures that you might document to accomplish the previously described spreadsheet application of customer acquisition could be as follows:

Step 1: Obtain a file or diskette containing customer purchases for the data period desired.

Step 2: Enter the customer purchase data into your workstation.

Step 3: Select the customer purchase analysis program from your application menu.

Step 4: Set program parameters to customers whose purchases decreased over $1,000 during the last month.

Step 5: List customers whose purchases are $1,000 less this month than they were last month.

Step 6: Follow up with customers in an attempt to secure more orders.

This simple procedure provides the basic information that the manager needs to perform the desired task. The amount of definition and narrative for each procedural step will depend on the experience you have in using the application package and the task you are performing. The more familiar you are with either the workstation or the manual support tasks, the less description you will need on how to perform each of the procedural steps.

Many people question the need for documenting and using procedures when the same task will be performed repetitively. The quality of work is normally increased, however, when procedures are used. For example, most pilots follow a documented procedure (i.e., a checklist) in preparation for landing their airplane. Occasionally those who don't find that they land with the wheels up. Developing and following procedures is good business practice that helps to avoid many of the "goofs" that are made on computers because the operator fails to perform an important step.

Area 3: Obtaining Assistance. The story of the pathfinder and the pioneer is well known. The pathfinder explored the rugged lands of the West and charted new courses, encountering many dangers. Many of the territories explored by the pathfinder were never known because that individual did not live to recount the exploits. However, the pathfinder was quickly followed by the pioneer, who rode the same path, but did not have nearly the same danger. These new areas inevitably were named after the pioneer, not the pathfinder.

Ask and you shall find out. Do not ask, and you might not know. These old adages are as applicable today as they were thousands of years ago. Investigation is one of the simplest, but frequently the most effective action you can take. Identify the individuals who have the knowledge you need, then get to know these people. The types of individuals who might be identified as potential workstation consultants include:

- Other workstation users in the same organization.
- Workstation users with similar job responsibilities in other organizations.
- Vendors of workstation hardware and software.
- Developers of workstation facilities.
- Consultants who work with workstations.
- Publications and services which evaluate technical capabilities.

The types of information that are obtainable through these people include:

- Performance statistics.
- Potential workstation capabilities.
- Vendors of good workstation products (e.g., software).
- Typical impediments to successful workstation performance.
- Tips and techniques to improve individual performance.
- Available education in the form of courses and books.
- Periodicals and reports on workstations, either industry-oriented or general.

Establishing your sources of information provides you with a procedure to get information, and to get out of trouble quickly.

Area 4: Sharing Knowledge. You need a procedure to share information with other people, who like you, are attempting to master technology in the day-to-day performance of a job. Many user groups use the slogan "birds of a feather" to indicate the gathering of people with like problems and interests. You should search out or organize a group of workstation users to share knowledge.

Data processing is an industry with a long history of users organizing to share information. Many of the user groups use names that indicate this sharing, such as SHARE, HUG, and GUIDE.

Some user groups are international, some local, others exist within industries, and some organize within a company. Wherever there is a group of individuals who can gain by sharing information among one another, a user group can be formed.

User groups tend to cluster around around common facilities such as vendor hardware and software products, industry uses of data processing resources, or common resources (e.g., workstations). They might also be organized by business activity. Frequently, two or more users get together to discuss common problems, and out of that discussion comes the user group. Several other users hear of this meeting, and ask to get together for lunch with the group. Soon the group meets regularly, and then they develop a more formal organization.

User groups also provide a power base to lobby for changes in automated facilities. For example, the users of early software organized to pressure the hardware vendors to produce better or different types of software. Within your organization, a user group can pressure management to develop new workstation capabilities.

DEVELOPING WORKSTATION PROCEDURES

Standardized processes enable less skilled people to succeed. Master craftsmen can create high-quality work using skills learned over many years. However, high-quality work can be performed by lesser craftsmen using a well-defined process. An artist can paint a beautiful scene on a blank canvas, an unskilled artist could paint a similar scene if the scene had been sketched out and the colors indicated by number. This analogy also applies to workstation processing.

A four-step process for identifying and developing workstation procedures is listed in Fig. 5-2.

Step 1: Develop a Task Baseline. A baseline of work tasks that will be performed on your workstation needs to be developed. If completed earlier, this listing of tasks can be used in this process. If not already done, you should develop that list now. This baseline represents the totality of work that might be transferred from the current method of processing to workstation processing.

Step 2: Identify Workstation Capabilities. This step requires listing tasks that can be performed on the workstation to be developed. The workstation capabilities should be expressed in terms consistent with your business needs using the list created in Step 1.

The capabilities listing might be more generic than your task listing. For example, a workstation capability could be spreadsheet processing, while your task would be to allocate sales costs among sales districts. It is important that your tasks (Step 1) be related to the workstation capabilities.

The identified capabilities should be business functions. These are sometimes referred to in data processing as *function points*. A function point represents a business product that is produced through automated processing. For example, to produce a report would be a function point, and to perform a complex calculation would also be considered a processing capability, or function point.

Step 3: Create a Tasks/Capabilities Matrix. At this point, you will have identified the portfolio of tasks transferable to the workstation, and the

Number	Step	Description	Responsibilities
1.	Develop task baseline.	Create (or use) a list of tasks needed to be performed by the user on the workstation (task identification, user groups).	° Workstation user
2.	Identify workstation capabilities	Create (or use) a list of processing capabilities provided by the workstation (investigation, data download, upload).	° Workstation developers
3.	Create tasks/ capabilities matrix.	Develop a matrix that crossreferences tasks to capabilities to identify mismatches.	° Workstation user
4.	Write workstation procedures.	Create the procedures to perform business tasks.	° Workstation user

Fig. 5-2. Ensuring adequate workstation capabilities.

workstation capabilities available to process those tasks. The objective of this step is to determine whether the tasks can be accomplished by the workstation capabilities. This can be done by creating a workstation task/capabilities matrix.

A sample matrix worksheet is shown in Fig. 5-3. The workstation tasks identified in Step 1 are listed on the horizontal axis of the matrix. The workstation capabilities identified in Step 2 are listed on the vertical axis. The intersection of the matrix indicates what tasks are performed using what capabilities.

The example shown is one in which a task can be accomplished by a stated workstation capability. In this example, the manager wants to allocate sales cost by sales district. Spreadsheet processing is indicated as the capability that can perform the task.

When there is a match between a task and a capability, the intersection between the two should be completed. The information included at the intersection will be dependent upon how the workstation capabilities are described. In this example, the capability is described as processing, in this case, spreadsheet processing. Therefore, the intersection contains the name of the spreadsheet processing software, Lotus 1-2-3.

If the workstation capabilities are vendor-oriented, for example, if the capability has been listed as Lotus 1-2-3, then the intersection would only require a check mark to indicate a capability that could perform a task. In some instances, more than one capability will be needed to perform a single work task. For example, if the workstation contained both Lotus 1-2-3 and VisiCalc, then both should be indicated as capable of performing the task listed in Fig. 5-3.

The completion of the matrix is a prerequisite to developing procedures. The successful completion of this step requires you to be knowledgeable in both workstation capabilities and the business tasks. Thus, you become the best-qualified person to complete the matrix. The previous step required you to become friendly with the workstation capabilities, so you should be able to quickly complete the matrix. However, you might want to consult with someone knowledgeable about workstation capabilities if you are unsure of any of them.

The matrix worksheet is used to assist in developing procedures by identifying the tasks which can and cannot be performed on the workstation, and determining the workstation capabilities that can be used to perform specific tasks. It can also be used to identify alternative processing means to perform tasks which cannot be done by the workstation. If capabilities don't exist, try to obtain them.

The tasks/capabilities matrix prepared in Step 3 identifies the missing capabilities. These are the intersections for which there is no capability to process the work described. The unfulfilled task list needs to be converted into workstation processing capabilities. This can be accomplished in the following manner:

- Develop a list of tasks from the matrix for which there are no capabilities.
- Arrange the tasks in a sequence so that all similar tasks are grouped together. For example, if many of the tasks involve allocating cost by certain factors, they could probably be handled by the same workstation capability.

Workstation Capabilities / Workstation Tasks	Allocate sales costs by sales district				
Spreadsheet processing	LOTUS 1-2-3				

Fig. 5-3. The workstation tasks/capabilities matrix worksheet.

In defining tasks, it is helpful to use the same verb (e.g., allocate) to indicate similar tasks.

- Generalize the group tasks. For example, you might generalize the tasks to say: "Allocate costs by several similar categories."
- Consult with the workstation development group to determine the types of capabilities that are available for processing your work requirements.

Once the list of capabilities has been identified, the plan for acquiring those capabilities can be developed. Two additional pieces of information are needed before the final plan is developed. The first is establishing the priority of the need for the capabilities. The workstation user should list the tasks in order of need. The second is information on the cost and availability of the needed capabilities. If needed capabilities are not readily available, the manager must inquire about the potential commercial availability in the near future, or the possibility of having it developed in-house.

The availability of new workstation capabilities will enable you to perform additional tasks on your workstation. If high-priority capabilities are unavailable, you might need to develop a plan to obtain them. The plan should be agreed upon by the workstation user and the individuals responsible for providing many of those capabilities. In some instances, the manager might take action to acquire some of the capabilities.

The plan for improving the workstation capabilities should include:

- An identification of each needed capability (if these are commercially available packages or hardware, the vendor and name of the capability should be described).
- The priority of the capability.
- The procedure that will be followed to acquire the capability, for example, acquisition, open bidding, or in-house development.
- Anticipated availability date of the new capability.
- Expected cost of the new capability.
- Method of paying for the capability, charged either to the user, to general overhead of the organization, or to a central function in charge of workstations.
- Responsibility to acquire the capability.
- Responsibility to install the capability.
- Criteria by which the success of the capability will be judged.
- Alternative course of action if the indicated capability fails to meet the success criteria established by the user (a commercially available package would be evaluated against these factors prior to acquisition).

Step 4: Write Workstation Procedures: A procedure is a step-by-step process for completing a task. The matrix, together with its analysis, indicates that parts of processing can be performed by the workstation, and what must be performed manually. If efforts to improve workstation capabilities fail or are delayed, the tasks for which there are no workstation capabilities must be performed manually. In addition, there are normally manual tasks to be done prior to, and following, workstation processing.

The procedures that need to be written define each of the steps that will be required to complete the business task. These can be prepared as simply and quickly as possible, because you might be the only user of those procedures. They are notes to guide you through performing a task.

A good written procedure has the following attributes:

- The procedure identifies the business tasks.
- The normal processing time is indicated, for example, monthly.
- The steps in the procedure begin when the business task starts, and continue until the business task is fully completed.
- The tasks are listed in the sequence in which they are to be performed.
- The tasks contain sufficient information, so that they can be performed without referencing other documents.
- Tasks that will not be performed by you are indicated, for example, as being performed by your secretary.
- Wherever possible, the entire procedure is recorded on a single sheet of paper.

All of your procedures should be filed in a single binder or folder. They should be referenced prior to performing a job, and, if the job is complex, used as a checklist to perform it.

IMPEDIMENTS AND COUNTERSTRATEGIES TO DEVELOPING WORKSTATION PROCEDURES

If the method to operate the workstation is easy and understandable, the business task will be accomplished quickly and effectively. One obvious question is: Why don't all managers follow the methodology described in this chapter to develop and document procedures? Things do not always happen the right way because individuals are involved in the process.

There are two major impediments associated with developing workstation procedures.

Impediment 1: Lack of Knowledge About Workstations. Workstations, to many people, are a significantly new way of doing work. Whatever is told them about workstations is what they believe. Many users fail to question the completeness or applicability of the capabilities provided, and do not inquire about capabilities that might be missing. An inquiring mind usually finds the answers.

The counterstrategy 1 is to know what is needed. Studying prior to writing procedures, is one of the strongest counterstrategies to failure. The educated user has a significantly higher probability of adapting the workstation capabilities to what is needed than the uneducated user. This education involves knowing what is needed before the procedure is developed. The difference between what is needed and what is offered should be the basis of questioning, designed to develop plans to close that gap.

Impediment 2: Failure of Users to Share Knowledge. A motto in many data processing organizations is: "If you must make a mistake, let it be a new one." In workstation usage, the same mistake is occurring over and over again because the information is not being shared. Managers are reluctant to advertise the fact that they are making mistakes, or that their workstations are not fully satisfying their needs. These problems are frequently viewed as weaknesses, rather than as opportunities to improve the workstation process.

The counterstrategy 2 involves forming user groups. Users must be provided with an opportunity to share information. This can be done through the formation of the user group, the issuance of a manager's workstation newsletter, or a central clearinghouse that establishes workstations. Managers should be provided a means, such as a problem definition form or a telephone number, to ensure that problem information can be recorded and disseminated to other users. Wherever known solutions are available for those problems, they should also be stated. The most common problems should be incorporated into training procedures and user manuals.

SELF-ASSESSMENT CHECKLIST

Self-assessment is not only an essential part of success, it adds to personal satisfaction. There is value in knowing that you have done well, or if not, why. The self-assessment is a checklist that helps people measure their performance, or the performance of the process against some norm of performance.

A checklist for evaluating the completeness of workstation procedures is provided as Fig. 5-4. This checklist is designed so that "yes" responses indicate effective procedures, and "no" answers identify potential procedural vulnerabilities. A comments column is provided for explanatory information that can be used in developing a plan to overcome problems.

Item	Response			
	Yes	No	N/A	Comments
1. Have you identified the needed tasks?				
2. Are the tasks described in sufficient detail so that they can be categorized by common processing capability?				
3. Are the identified tasks consistent with your processing baseline developed in Chapter 2?				
4. Have the workstation capabilities been identified?				
5. Have you conducted sufficient investigation to know what type of capabilities are available for workstations?				
6. Has a facility been established to enable users to interact with one another regarding workstation uses and capabilities?				

7. Do users know the types of data available in the central data processing function?					
8. Have capabilities been included to download central data to workstations?					
9. Have the capabilities been created to permit data to be uploaded from workstations to central sites?					
10. Can workstations transmit data among themselves?					
11. Have you matched the available capabilities against the needed tasks (i.e., a tasks/capabilities matrix)?					
12. Have the missing capabilities been identified?					
13. Has a plan been developed to acquire those missing capabilities?					
14. Have the items within the plan been prioritized so that the most-needed capabilities will be acquired first?					
15. Have you accepted the responsibility to develop your own procedures?					
16. Do the procedures include both the manual and workstation tasks?					
17. Are the procedures oriented toward accomplishing business tasks?					
18. Do the procedures reference specific workstation capabilities?					
19. Do the procedures indicate tasks that are being performed by individuals other than yourself?					
20. Are the procedures documented in a common format (note that this can be a hand-written format)?					
21. Are all the procedures filed in a common area for ready reference?					
22. Do you intend to use the procedures to help you execute each business task?					
23. Will you update the procedures each time the processes change to perform a business task?					

Fig. 5-4. The workstation capabilities self-assessment checklist.

WORKSTATION RULE OF THUMB
Identifying needed procedures and developing them is the best method to ensure your tasks will be performed correctly.

Chapter 6

Action 4: House the Workstation Befitting Its Rank

Neither managers nor workstations are created equal. A senior manager's workstation should look like a senior manager's workstation, not a secretarial pool unit. Not only must the capabilities be managerial, but the office equipment and layout supporting the workstation must also say, "It's a manager's workstation."

This chapter explains the importance of office space to workstation performance. Both the functional and social issues of office design are discussed. The strategies and methods that should be used in building a highly functional and aesthetically pleasing workstation for a manager's office are presented. The chapter describes the impediments to doing this, and concludes with a self-assessment checklist for evaluating the effectiveness of office layouts.

When you acquire a new piece of furniture for your home, you place it in an existing group of furniture. The result is that the new item looks out of place with the old furniture. Placing a new television on the old television stand might make economic sense, but would not be effective if the old stand is large and the new set is small. Pennies saved in reusing furniture might cost dollars in lost productivity.

The layout and equipment needed to effectively utilize the workstation might conflict with the existing building systems, office furnishings, office layout, and the social aspects of office design. The result will be managers and professional workstation users who:

- Do not use the equipment.
- Do not use the equipment efficiently and effectively.
- Do not become proficient in operating the equipment.
- Do not meet the projected gains in performance.

Many organizations are not sensitive to the housing requirements for workstation equipment. The simple answer is to "park" a piece of equipment on existing furniture. The result is not only an aesthetically displeasing office, but it might result in a nonfunctional office.

GOOD-LOOKING OFFICES ARE MORE THAN STATUS SYMBOLS

An office is a very personal part of an individual's work life. The mementos included in an office, the personalization of the office, and the way that a person arranges work all affect that person's productivity. Depersonalizing someone's office is recognized as a mistake. Although standardizing offices is a common practice, workstation designers should avoid this practice.

One organization, in an attempt to make all offices look alike, passed an edict that no personal pictures or mementos could be placed on office walls. The company provided the pictures that could be used. This greatly distressed one manager, who regarded his individuality as important. That manager, in defiance of this rule, hung the American flag on the wall. His argument was that it was not personal but, rather, a symbol of his country. It took several meetings of high-level executives to decide whether the flag could remain. The result was an exception to the company policy, allowing flags to be hung on the wall. The disruption caused by forcing conformity caused losses in productivity.

Managers normally used their available space carefully. The way they use it is usually important to them. For example, arrangements of piles of paper might indicate the type and quantity of work to be done. If workstation equipment disrupts normal work habits, it could result in lower manager productivity. Therefore, redesigning offices for workstations should take into account personal work patterns. Items that are unimportant to an outsider might be essential elements of productivity to the manager. The skilled layout artist is attuned to these managerial idiosyncracies and builds work space to accommodate them. The objective of good office layout procedures is to improve productivity, not to minimize one-time expenditures of furniture and to build look-alike offices.

The science of ergonomics has been established to address the problems of modern office efficiency. Ergonomic principles indicate that the positioning of the keyboard, the coloring of the video screen, and the ease of combining the capabilities of two or more physical facilities into a single unit all affect productivity. In many instances, attention to ergonomics makes the difference between using a workstation and not using it. The more inconvenient the office layout is to the user, the less likely it is that the new facilities will be used.

The challenges that must be faced in adapting a manager's office to workstation processing include:

- Satisfying the manager's personal need for individuality.
- Creating a highly functional work area.
- Creating an aesthetically pleasing work area.
- Minimizing the cost of creating a work area.
- Matching the characteristics of the office to the attributes that make workstation equipment physically easy to use.
- Providing the manager with adequate privacy in which to use and experiment with new office technology.

WORKSTATION RULE OF THUMB
The impact of office layout on productivity must not be overlooked. A few dollars spent in the office might provide a huge productivity gain in return.

THE CHARACTERISTICS OF GOOD OFFICE LAYOUT

The people who do the office layout require training and an understanding of the ergonomic principles of an effective office. It involves much more than merely ordering and arranging office equipment. Not only must it address the physical organization of the office to promote efficiency and productivity, but it must also meet the needs of the individual and the organization. Office layout, however, is not entitled to an unlimited budget. There must be a realistic consideration of costs, consistent with the position of the individual. Many companies want the offices of the senior managers to be furnished in a slightly better decor than those of the junior managers.

The five attributes of the automated office are the building system, the office furnishings, the total package of workstation equipment, the office layout, and the social aspects of the office. Each of these five factors is important to managerial productivity. The effective office designer takes into consideration all five characteristics when designing an office space.

The five characteristics will be constrained by organizational procedures and budgets. For example, procedures might indicate the type of office furniture appropriate for different pay grades. Budgets might establish limits on the amount of funds that can be expended. Office designers, working within these organizational constraints should take into account the five characteristics.

Office Characteristic 1: Building Systems. Some aspects of buildings can be changed and others can't. The four most important aspects that are adjustable include power, heating and cooling, lighting, and noise level. Failure to address any of these four building system characteristics can affect productivity.

Electronic equipment is subject to errors when power fluctuates. Lightning, loss of power, or other events that cause an uneven voltage supply can cause errors and loss of computer processing. At a minimum, power supplies should be equipped with a power surge device to monitor and help ensure an even power supply.

Office equipment generates heat. It is the equivalent of adding more people to a work space, which in warmer times might require additional cooling for the comfort of individuals. Even if equipment can operate effectively at higher temperatures, people might not be able to do so. It becomes important in offices that have electronic equipment to be able to control the heat and cooling facilities within that area.

Room illumination is extremely important when video displays are used. Offices with video displays require different lighting treatment than traditional offices. Glare might make screens difficult to read and cause eyestrain.

Office equipment generates noise that can rapidly pollute the working environment of the manager using that equipment. Noise not only affects the individual doing the work, but might affect the productivity of individuals in surrounding office space. Special noise-reduction materials should be used if noisy equipment, such as printers, are in use.

Business systems that are inappropriately designed for automated office technology might lead to complaints and loss in productivity. Executives consistently complain about working environments not properly attuned to their needs. The result of poor office planning might be the abandonment of the workstation.

Office Characteristic 2: Furnishings. Every major office furniture manufacturer produces a line of furniture designed for electronic office equipment. This furniture is specifically tailored to provide adjustable heights, angles, and swivels for electronic equipment, such as data entry keyboards.

Many organizations, when they issue workstation hardware, just place the electronic devices on top of the manager's desk. This results in physical complaints such as eyestrain, backaches, and neckaches. These problems are directly related to improperly designed furniture for the use of electronic equipment. When automated equipment is added to an executive's office, new "systems" furniture should also be added. This cost is small in relationship to the benefits. Not only is the practice of using existing office furniture unsound, but it reduces the existing work areas. This can be particularly wasteful when the workstation is only used a small percent of the time.

WORKSTATION RULE OF THUMB
New "systems" furniture should be considered an integral part of the workstation, so that the office equipment is never ordered separately from the furniture with which it will be used.

Office Characteristic 3: Workstation Automated Equipment.
The ergonomic aspects of automated equipment should be considered when acquiring the equipment. For example, the angle of the video screen, the movement and ease of using a keyboard, the position of keys, and the physical closeness of equipment should all be evaluated. Most workstation equipment is now built using ergonomic principles.

Office Characteristic 4: Office Layout. In electronic offices, the physical layout of the office refers not only to the plan inside an individual office, but the relationship among workstations. For example, managers' workstations might be coupled to secretarial and other support workstations. Thus, not only is the physical distance important, but the interconnecting of equipment gains importance.

Studies have shown that face-to-face contact in organizations falls off sharply when people are located at distances over 150 feet apart. The contact falls off more quickly if there are obstructions between individuals. This has two implications. First, the need for electronic communication between individuals over 150 feet apart, and second, facilities that are located over 150 feet from a user will not be used extensively. For example, if a shared printer requires an individual to walk over 150 feet, the number of items printed will be decreased. This phenomenon also exists with copy machines and other office equipment.

The physical workstation must be designed to minimize movement of the individual performing tasks. This normally requires that the workstation be readily accessible, and near to work space where the individual can perform manual, but related, tasks. Much of this layout requires study of people movement. Most office equipment and furniture manufacturers provide model layouts to minimize work movement and improve personal productivity. If your organization's office designers are not trained in ergonomics, many vendors of office equipment and furniture will provide a recommended office design for you.

Office Characteristic 5: Social Aspects. The two major social issues are status and "turf." Depending on who uses workstations and how they are allocated, the use of a workstation might be either a positive or negative status symbol. If the president uses a workstation, it can be considered a positive status symbol, but if workstations are currently the domain of the clerical staff, then providing the manager a workstation might be a negative status symbol.

The ownership of the workstation, and the facilities provided, help define one's working turf. The intangibles associated with workstations become as important as the office with a window, a rug on the floor, a plant watered by a gardener, a table with three chairs, an underground parking space, or any other symbol awarded by the organization as representative of status. Many of these symbols are coveted as much as pay increases, and might have more effect on productivity and feeling of importance.

It is important that you understand these characteristics of good office layout, otherwise, you might be provided with ineffective capabilities. You should not assume that the individual designing a workstation-centered office understands the close relationship between productivity and the layout of the office. Understanding the characteristics that will improve your productivity with workstation processing can enable you to intelligently participate in the new layout of your office.

OFFICE LAYOUT STRATEGIES

Recognizing layout deficiencies does not qualify you to solve that problem. However, the application of managerial principles to the problem will lead you to the solution.

The managerial strategies that can be used to ensure the adequacy of an office arrangement for workstation usage are listed in Fig. 6-1.

Strategy 1: Engage Consultants. Good managerial strategy implies that the manager buy the best talent available to solve specific business problems. It is another instance in which "penny wise and pound foolish" costs the organization. The price paid for a consultant might be minimal compared to the benefits gained from a few hours or days of evaluation and advice.

The source of individuals to perform office layout consulting includes office layout consultants, furniture and office equipment vendors, industrial psychologists, and office planning firms. In some instances, the consulting comes free. For example, if you acquire office "systems" furniture from a large business furniture vendor, that vendor frequently has office consultants to help lay out office space. Many of these consultants will come to your place of business and propose office layouts as part of the service of dealing with that vendor. In other instances, consultants might be quite expensive.

If office layout is infrequently performed, or the use of workstations is a new concept, then consultants might be advisable. Even if the expertise appears to be in-house, a confirmation of correctness might be an economical safety factor. One of the strongest of all managerial controls is redundancy.

Number	Strategy	Description
1.	Engage consultants.	Utilizes the advice and recommendations of an expert to select and/or review office layouts.
2.	Learn about ergonomics.	The science of matching furniture and equipment to the needs of specific individuals.
3.	Develop a usage	Identify when and for how long the workstation will be used by the manger.
4.	Protect privacy/security.	Recognize the importance of providing the workstation user with adequate privacy and security.

Fig. 6-1. Office layout strategies.

In other words, if you perform the same task twice using different methods and then compare results, it helps you determine whether the results are correct. In mathematics, multiplication can be used to prove the correctness of division. This is a redundant exercise, but significantly increases the probability that the answer will be correct. Having a consultant evaluate needs and propose a solution is redundant, if it is the same result as proposed internally, but the manager has a much higher probability that the proposed results will be correct.

It is advisable to operate under two ground rules when using a consultant. First, the consulting objective should be clearly established, so that both the organization and consultant will know when the engagement has been successfully completed. Second, the consultant should not be told what the organization believes is the appropriate conclusion but, rather, require the consultant to come up with an independent recommendation before comparing it to what any in-house office management group has proposed.

Strategy 2: Learn About Ergonomics Ergonomics is a relatively new science designed to match the physical architecture of equipment and furniture to the functions of individuals. The science recognizes that there is a relationship between physical comfort and productivity.

You only need to study the practices of data entry operators to learn some of the effects of ergonomics. In the early days of data processing, data entry forms were designed without consultation or concern about the needs of the data entry operators. Management quickly found that forms improperly designed from a key entry perspective caused the data entry operators to make significantly more keying errors than in applications where the forms were designed to optimize the key entry operation. This lesson can be extended to the lighting, location of equipment, relationship of equipment to work products, and so forth.

To design a workstation environment without considering the science of ergonomics would be like designing a building without using the services of an architect. Certainly an individual could design his own home, but the inefficiency of that home, and its cost, might be significantly higher than if the services of an architect were engaged, using the building sciences.

Ergonomics have significantly changed the architecture of workstation equipment. When the equipment was first produced, the keyboards were physically attached to the terminal because it made sense from a manufacturing and cost perspective. However, the bulkiness of the unit did not permit the proper separation of the keyboard from the view of the terminal. Either the equipment was not at eye level or it was inconvenient to use the keyboard. Ergonomics principles convinced manufacturers of the desirability of separating the two components. Office furniture design also followed these principles, and we now have desks with different levels for locating keyboards lower than the display equipment.

There are many articles and books written on the science of ergonomics. It would be unwise to engage a consultant who was not a student of ergonomics, or to let an internal office staff member who does not understand the ergonomic principles develop workstation offices. This expertise is a must to ask of those individuals designing office layout.

WORKSTATION RULE OF THUMB
The science of ergonomics is an essential principle for designing automated office workstations. Office designers who are not students of this new science should not be employed.

Strategy 3: Develop a Usage Baseline. A usage baseline is a profile of expected use of the workstation. The profile should indicate the following:

- Percent of time the workstation will be used.
- The extent of the workstation usage, preferably by time and day.
- Type of applications, detailing what aspects of workstation processing will be used.
- Expected changes in frequency of use, and factors that could affect expected usage.

This usage baseline information is an important factor in designing the office layout. For example, a workstation that will only be used fifteen minutes a day does not require the same planning and attention as a workstation that will be in use three hours a day. It is also important to know whether the usage will be in a single block of time, in which case it might be possible for the manager to move to another location, or whether the workstation will be used periodically throughout the day. For example, the manager might need to use the workstation during telephone conversations, or during the preparation or interpretation of reports.

The required information should be collected through interviews by the individuals designing or rearranging office space. If those individuals fail to collect this information, you should ask why. However, you should ensure that the information you give will be used by the office design staff.

Strategy 4: Ensure Privacy and Security. Privacy and security are important managerial factors. The design of the equipment and the associated support furniture should be conducive to providing privacy and security. These are closely related but separate issues.

Privacy in workstation processing is needed from two perspectives. First, the type of information and analyses being done might need to be shielded from other individuals in the organization, or passers-by. Privacy might also be needed to permit the manager to experiment and make mistakes without observation by third parties.

Security is an organizational responsibility. The manager is a part of the security program. The manager has a responsibility to protect the information for which he or she is a custodian. The design of the workstation facility, both physical and logical, must take into account this security, and provide the user with the necessary security tools.

ENSURING ADEQUATE OFFICE LAYOUT

Much of the responsibility for the design of the workstation office will reside with the staff assigned that layout responsibility. On the other hand, you, the manager, should not entrust your destiny to a third party. You have a vested interest in your office design, because it will affect your personal productivity.

The four steps that help you survive the office layout exercise are listed in Fig. 6-2. The strategies are included in brackets at the end of the description column, and the person responsible for the step is in the responsibilities column. Note that these people have the primary responsibility, which does not exclude you from providing input into these steps.

Step 1: Identify Personal Space Requirements. Your personal office space is too important to leave to the discretion of an office design person. The person designing the office will do the job and leave. You, as the user of the workstation-equipped office, will have to live with that design for many months, or even years. The design process offers an opportunity for you to provide input to the design process.

Good office design procedures should provide for an office design specialist interviewing you to determine your personal likes and dislikes. This does not mean that you will receive every office amenity desired, but, rather, that your personal considerations should be taken into account when the office is designed and the equipment selected. Even in organizations with rather rigid office standards, there is room for flexibility.

The types of individual customization can include:

- Equipment and furniture designed for right-handed or left-handed people.
- Office habits regarding workspace, filing, and document retention.
- Need for privacy and security (particularly job-related needs).
- Physical attributes of the user, such as height, arm reach, and eyesight.
- Preferences in color.
- Preferences in style of equipment.
- Frequency and types of meetings conducted in office (especially those that require workstation capabilities).

These items are typical of those contained on checklists for office designers. If the office layout designers fail to ask you these types of questions, you should raise these issues regarding what options are available to you.

Step 2: Identify Workstation Equipment. The equipment available might be preselected, or there might be equipment options available. The types of equipment and office furniture will depend on the defined processing

Number	Step	Description	Responsibilities
1.	Identify personal space requirements.	Define personal desires for equipment, furniture, color, design, and other factors of personal preference (ergonomics, develop a usage baseline).	○ Workstation user
2.	Identify workstation equipment.	Determine what equipment (including furniture) is available for office layout (ergonomics, engage consultant).	○ Workstation developers
3.	Identify attributes of an efficient office layout.	Determine the attributes of an effective office (ergonomics, engage consultants, protect privacy/security).	○ Office manager
4.	Redesign workspace for workstation usage.	Lay out the needed equipment and furniture with the available office restrictions to maximize use and productivity (ergonomics, engage consultants, develop a usage baseline, protect privacy/security).	○ Workstation user ○ Workstation developers ○ Office manager

Fig. 6-2. Ensuring adequate office layout.

requirements, the desire for standardization, and the budget of the organization.

In some organizations, there is a variety of available equipment, from which you can choose. The workstation equipment considerations should include:

- Terminals and keyboards.
- Communication facilities.
- Supporting equipment, such as disk drives.
- Auxiliary equipment, such as microfilm/microfiche readers.
- Storage facilities for computer media. The type of equipment will depend on the need for security.
- Sound control equipment, if necessary.

Step 3: Identify Attributes of an Efficient Office Layout. Good office design doesn't just happen. It is not a process of arranging furniture and equipment until it looks good. Office engineering needs to be preplanned and built around the science of ergonomics.

This step is designed to ensure that those responsible for office design are appropriately qualified for that function. In larger organizations, this might not be a problem, and the step might not need to be performed. Smaller organizations, or organizations without adequate internal expertise, might need to acquire that expertise from outside.

An earlier part of this chapter defined five attributers of good office design. These attributes provide the framework around which offices should be structured. You must be involved in the design of your office layout. Without the proper attention to office design, the amount of grumbling and complaints about using the workstation will be high.

Step 4: Redesign Workspace for Workstation Usage. The actual office layout is a culmination of the previous three steps. The point that warrants emphasizing in this step is the need to develop a formal layout diagram. Office design personnel have special worksheets and tools designed for this purpose.

You should review and approve the layout. If it is built using the information collected in Steps 1 and 2, and designed in accordance with the attributes identified in Step 3, the actual design should be efficient and quickly approved.

GOOD OFFICE LAYOUT:
IMPEDIMENTS AND COUNTERSTRATEGIES

Good office layouts are so important that you would think that office layout would not be a major problem. Unfortunately, it is. Office design is too frequently viewed as just providing the needed equipment and furniture, rather than customizing that workspace for you. The impediments that cause poor office design are listed below, together with the counterstrategies for overcoming those impediments.

Impediment 1: Company Policy and Procedure. Frequently, office layout procedures are designed to provide equal equipment for equal pay grades. The emphasis is more on equality than functionality. When the procedure states that pay grade X gets certain furniture, it doesn't matter whether that furniture is conducive to workstation processing or not, it's what an individual of that pay grade gets.

The counterstrategy is to redesign office layout and furnishing procedures to take into account workstation technology. What was reasonable before the advent of workstations might not be reasonable today. You should challenge the application of policies and procedures related to manual paper shuffling in a workstation environment.

Impediment 2: We've Always Done It That Way. Tradition is important in many organizations. If the office manager has always selected equipment, the office manager will continue to do that. You must recognize when something is proposed for the office just because "we have always done it that way." When you challenge tradition, you might need a strong argument to create change.

The counterstrategy is to initiate new traditions. Traditions need to change with time. Just as policies and procedures must change, so must the methods. It is important that you identify the causes of change, and then present them to the "powers that be" so that the appropriate methods and traditions can change.

Impediment 3: Desire to Reuse Existing Equipment. This is a money-saving impediment—"We own the furniture, why not use it?"

The counterstrategy applies the principles of ergonomics to organizations. New furniture must be selected because of the benefits produced through increased managerial productivity. A well-thought-through argument should convince the decision makers that the cost of furniture designed for office systems is a cost they cannot afford not to incur.

Impediment 4: Lack of Office Layout Knowledge. This impediment is one of ignorance. Management has the responsibility to train their staff in how to perform their job functions. People cannot do a job for which they have not been trained.

As a counterstrategy use consultants. If the needed skills are not in existence in the organization, then the organization should buy those skills from consultants.

SELF-ASSESSMENT CHECKLIST

The survivors in office automation are the ones who challenge the methods by which that automation is introduced and utilized. The inquiring mind is an important mind to have in the organization. The self-assessment checklist for the office layout is provided in Fig. 6-3. This checklist is designed so that "yes" responses indicate good office layout practices, while "no" answers present potential productivity vulnerabilities. The "no" responses should be investigated and resolved before the layout is approved.

WORKSTATION RULE OF THUMB
The layout of your office space is too important to leave to the discretion of another individual.

Item	Response			
	Yes	No	N/A	Comments
1. Is the science of ergonomics used in office layout?				
2. Do the office designers take into account the personal desires of the individual who will occupy the office?				
3. Is the power supply adjusted so that a continuous voltage of power will be supplied (e.g., the use of a power surge adapter)?				
4. Can you control the temperature within the office with a thermostat?				
5. Have measures been provided to reduce the sound if it is a pollutant characteristic?				
6. Is room illumination adjusted so that terminal screens can be easily read (without glare)?				
7. Is a line of "systems" furniture used in conjunction with workstations?				
8. Has adequate workspace been provided in the office?				
9. Has adequate storage space been provided?				
10. Is the storage space consistent with security requirements?				
11. Has the office furniture and equipment been aligned to accommodate personal physical characteristics?				
12. Is the office space aesthetically pleasing to the eye?				
13. Is the design of the furniture desirable to the individual?				
14. Are the office colors conducive with good work habits?				
15. Is the office design based on the frequency and extent of use of workstation equipment?				
16. Is the office consistent with the status of the individual who will occupy the office?				
17. Is the office work area adequately protected from intrusion?				
18. Are the use of consultants considered where appropriate?				
19. Is the budget for the office redesign consistent with ergonomic prinicples?				
20. Is the occupant of the office pleased with the new design?				
21. Has the occupant of the office been consulted regarding personal desires?				

Fig. 6-3. The office layout self-assessment checklist.

Chapter 7

Action 5: Feed the Workstation with Information

Workstations are a product of the information age. They use and create information. Satisfying the appetite for information, and using the information produced by the workstation are important ingredients in workstation effectiveness.

This chapter addresses the challenge of obtaining information for your workstation processing. Most of this information will come from either centralized databases or business colleagues. The availability of that information will depend on both the procedures established at central sites for disseminating information, and your personal initiative to identify and obtain useful information.

Workstations are creating a new challenge called "information starvation." The phenomenon is due to the fact that there is a mushrooming of automated equipment in many companies. With commercially available software, and low-priced hardware, the acquisition of computer processing is easy. However, once that processing unit is acquired, its usefulness is based upon the availability of information. The gathering, recording, entry, and organization of data for computer processing is a time-consuming process. Managers who might have the initiative and time to do computer processing probably do not have the time to initiate and organize the necessary files. Data is needed from sources other than you entering it via a keyboard.

THE INFORMATION RELIABILITY CHALLENGE

The staff of your centralized data processing department has spent years learning how to ensure the *reliability* of information. Reliability means that the automated information is accurate and complete enough so that the user can rely on that information for decision-making purposes. Reliability procedures include elaborate data validation routines, electronic labels that identify certain types of information, internal control totals which continually check to ensure that the detailed data within a file equals the control total, and frequency checks to externally maintained control totals.

The cost of data collection and data validation is one of the major costs of the centralized data processing function. Programs in computer applications that validate input data are among the largest and most complex systems in commercial data processing systems. It is important to recognize the cost and effort that must be expended in order to ensure the reliability of data.

Many individuals, in using workstations, obtain and enter data into workstation storage. That information might have only minimal validation procedures applied before being used for processing. The results of that processing are then used to make decisions. In some cases, the information and recommendations based on that information are passed to higher levels of management for action.

The fact that many workstation users minimize the reliability assessment of data can result in poor management decisions. For example, in one company, an inventory manager did an analysis of sales, concluded that some products were significantly understocked, and recommended large inventory replenishment orders. It was only a last-minute challenge by senior management that led the inventory manager to recognize that he had processed monthly sales as weekly sales, showing significantly inflated purchasing. Had the mistake not been caught, the company would have significantly overstocked its inventory, experienced large storage costs, and might have acquired inventory which could not be sold.

The challenge that you, as a workstation user, face is how to ensure the reliability and integrity of the data you are processing on your equipment. The two options available to you are to install data validation processes similar to those in the central site, or to acquire data from a source which has performed those data validation procedures. Obviously, the most desirable choice is to acquire information from a source that can guarantee the reliability and integrity of data.

STRATEGIES FOR ACQUIRING RELIABLE INFORMATION

Workstations without information are worthless. Therefore, organizations must undertake those strategies needed to ensure a steady stream of information to workstation users.

The five strategies that are recommended for ensuring a steady stream of information to workstation processing are listed in Fig. 7-1.

Strategy 1: Data Dictionary. You should validate your data in accor-

Number	Strategy	Description
1.	Data dictionary specifications	A software documentation tool designed for the purpose of describing data and the attributes of that data.
2.	Company databases	Collections of data accessible by multiple users concurrently—available to workstations via communication capabilities.
3.	Download/upload procedures	The methods used to transfer data between central sites and workstations, and between workstations.
4.	Commercial databases	Commercially available collections of data, for example, a stock price database.
5.	Other workstation data	Data accumulated by other workstations for which the validity has been verified.

Fig. 7-1. Workstation information acquisition strategies.

dance with the validity rules in your company's *data dictionary*. (Not all companies have a data dictionary, but they all have documentation on data validity.) A data dictionary is a software tool used to document elements of data and the attributes of that data. It, like any other dictionary, provides a ready reference of information about data. A common definition in the data dictionary provides a means of communication between individuals about the data used in your organization. This definition defines the tests the data must pass to be considered valid.

Different users of data might refer to the same piece of data in many different ways. For example, a data element might be called a social security number by one user, but that same number, used to identify employees, might also be known as an employee number. The question to the workstation user would be whether this is one or two pieces of data. In real life, the confusion is much greater than with this simple example.

The objective of the data dictionary is twofold: first, to provide a ready reference of common data definitions, and second, to enforce those definitions through software. Most companies have only reached the first objective, but only a few have enforced those definitions by requiring users to access data through standardized definitions documented in the data dictionary.

In an information processing environment, the data dictionary is considered one of the strongest controls. It is difficult for an organization to have information managed as a resource until there is a common definition for that information. In the early days of electronic data processing, data was "owned" by the application that used it. Therefore, it made little difference whether application A and application B called the same piece of data by the same name, or whether it met the same validity requirements. However, as applications became more integrated, and third-party users, such as workstation users, became involved in the use of common information, the need for common definitions and common validity increased.

You can use the data dictionary as a source of information about data. A look through the data dictionary will familiarize you with the definition and validity rules for the information your company uses. The detailed descriptions will explain where the data is used, what files are available, and the attributes of information. This detailed explanation will provide you with the types of analysis that you must perform on data before you can consider it valid and reliable. For example, you might have to check the range of values of a data element, and verify control totals.

Strategy 2: Company Databases. Databases are groupings of data managed by an individual, independent of the applications that use them. In conventional data processing, the same individual who develops the processing creates the information. In this context, the application owns the data that it uses.

In database processing, data is broken apart from processing. One group originates and maintains the data, while another group develops the programs and processes the data. This is made possible by a software package called a database management system (DBMS).

A database management system is a single piece of software that controls data independently of the applications that use it. The DBMS is a true manager which directs or manages the use of data by multiple applications. The actual mechanical work involved in using the data is performed by another facility. The actual work might be considered to be performed by the DBMS staff. A database provides the following advantages to an organization:

• Permits more than one application to access the same data concurrently. This eliminates the need to create redundant files for various processing applications.

• Manages data at the data element level. Both security and control can be provided at this level. This means that access to the database does not require access to all the data in the database. With a file used exclusively by a single program, that program has access to all the information in the file. In a database environment, access is only for those data elements needed.

• Information is retrievable in almost any sequence. Database capabilities permit access of the database through multiple sequences. For example, a file of employees might be accessible by employee number, social security number, employee department, employee skill, or other attribute. Also, while one application is accessing data in a database by employee number, another can be searching it by employee skill.

Databases are normally organized by homogeneous areas. These frequently center around business cycles, such as inventory, revenue, expenditures, personnel, and financial databases.

Workstations rarely use entire databases; they more commonly use segments of databases. If your workstation can be connected to the central computer site, you can access and use data stored in your company's databases.

The reliability of this data has already been ensured by your central data processing function.

Strategy 3: Download/Upload Procedures. The mechanics of getting data from a centralized area to a workstation (downloading) and vice versa (uploading) is complex, although it might appear to be a simple matter of transferring or physically moving data from one location to another.

Workstations have size and processing restrictions. These restrictions include:

- Size of disk storage areas.
- Data element size.
- Data element attributes.
- Record size.
- Number of fields in a record.

If the information from the central site varies from what the workstation can process, the data is worthless. Thus, data conversion routines are frequently needed to convert data from one format to another. Because these conversion routines are not readily available, they need to be built in-house. This requires the availability of the appropriate resources.

The transmission of data in the opposite direction—from the workstation to a central site—has exactly the same problems. This, too, normally requires a conversion routine, but this time converting from a format usable by workstation processing into the common data definition attributes described in the data dictionary.

Some workstations only have limited value until these downloading and uploading procedures are developed. Few managers can afford the time and effort to enter large amounts of data for processing purposes. Thus, the capabilities of the workstation become limited until the information needed can be delivered to the workstation.

The movement of data to and from the central site can be performed by procedures designed to upload and download that data. This requires reformatting to meet the processing needs of the receiver or sender, because the format of data used for workstation processing might be significantly different than that used in the central site. For example, there might be size differences in the length of the field. In downloading, not only might formatting be needed, but processes might need to be developed to extract only those data elements or records needed by the workstation.

Strategy 4: Commercial Databases. A few years ago, most data had to be created, entered, and maintained by the company that used it. Now, more and more databases are offered for sale by vendors. These can be used to process information such as stock prices, commodity prices, and financial and product reports. Some businesses now make their data available to their customers. For example, insurance companies will provide diskettes about employees of your company covered by their programs, such as pension programs; and vendors might provide you with lists of their products so that you will have ready access to price and descriptions. Even many banks are now permitting organizations to access records in the bank databases, to inquire about transactions processed by the bank and to move funds among the company's accounts.

Strategy 5: Other Workstation Data. As more and more managers begin processing data on workstations, they build their own data files. If those managers take the time and effort to carefully record and validate the data, those files can be made available to other users. For example, if you were a marketing manager and an accounts receivable manager had data about your customers, having access to that data might save you the trouble of entering that data into your own workstation files.

The concern in transmitting data from user to user is the degree of reliability that can be placed on data obtained from other users. Sometimes this information is processed through user groups which will either establish ground rules for validity, or independently do checks to ensure the validity of data before it is passed to other users.

IDENTIFYING SOURCES OF RELIABLE INFORMATION

Knowing the strategies available for ensuring the reliability is not enough. You also need to know specific sources. Few organizations have developed inventories of information. This is because information is not considered an asset of an organization, and thus does not merit the control that it would if it was considered an asset. Therefore, you might have to do some investigation to determine who has the information that you need.

This process is not normally complex. For example, if you are looking for accounts receivable information, you would go to the accounts receivable department to find out who has it. User groups sometimes have records of the type of processing performed by different users. Normally, with two or three telephone calls, you can determine whether the data that you need is available. A four-step process for locating data is listed in Fig. 7-2.

Step 1: Identify Information Needed For Job Responsibilities. You might find it difficult to break jobs down into lists of data elements needed for each process. However, if the methodologies described earlier in this book have been followed, you should currently have a list of your job tasks. This step involves identifying the specific data elements or records associated with each of those tasks.

This is the same process followed by the systems analyst in designing systems. One of the first tasks the analyst does is to identify the data used by an application system. Input data for the system must be created. Output data can be a combination of the input data passed through processing, or new or modified data elements created during processing.

Number	Step	Description	Responsibility
1.	Identify information needed for job responsibilities.	Determine what data elements, records, and files will be needed for workstation processing (data dictionary, information inventory, chief information officer).	○ Workstation user
2.	Identify custodian of the needed information.	Determine who can authorize release of the data to the user of a workstation (chief information officer or staff).	○ Database administrator
3.	Negotiate the acquisition of the needed information.	Take those measures necessary to obtain and use the needed data (chief information officer).	○ Information custodian
4.	Personally generate new information.	Create the information that is not readily available (database, download/upload procedures).	○ Workstation user

Fig. 7-2. Methods to provide information.

Determining the information needed for each job responsibility is a three-task process. The first task is to obtain a listing of all of the job tasks that will be performed on your workstation. The second task involves identifying all of the output work products that will be produced by your workstation. If possible, these should be mockups of actual output reports or displays on a video screen. Each of the data elements on the report or the screen should be identified. The final task is to identify and list the data elements that will be needed to produce the output reports. Note that some of the output data elements are calculations from, or combinations of, input data. This listing of input data will be the information needed to fulfill the manager's job responsibility.

Because the workstation opens new processing opportunities for you, you should not only consider what has been done in the past, but also consider what might be done in the future. Suggestions for this can be obtained by reviewing the data available in the data dictionary and interviewing individuals knowledgeable in the types of information used by your business.

Step 2: Identify Custodian of the Needed Information. Although information is owned by the organization, it is usually in the custody of a single individual or department which has the responsibility and control over the information. You must identify that individual or department in order to request access to or copies of the information in their custody.

The procedures needed to use information vary from company to company. Some companies are very open about the use of their information, while others require special permission and/or passwords to access the data. Most organizations with a centralized data processing function have someone in that group responsible for data security. You should talk to that individual about accessing corporate databases.

Step 3: Negotiate the Acquisition of the Needed Information. Acquisition of information is a two-part process. The first part is to obtain access to use the information. The second part is to acquire the information in a format that will be usable by your workstation capabilities.

Access to information is rarely denied if a good reason to know can be established. Therefore, you should first determine why you need access to the information and, second, request permission for that information. The well-prepared individual succeeds. The acquisition of information in a format that is readily usable is the most difficult task. This requires that you know both the existing format of data, and the format in which the workstation programs need the data. In some instances, however, central sites will already have handled this transition.

One of the major concerns about sharing central data with distributed users is that of security. The argument is that once the data is placed in the hands of the workstation user, control over that information is lost. However, this concept is no different than when that same user was given a printed report of data from the central site. The rules on security for workstations should be basically the same as that used to protect a printed report.

Step 4: Personally Generate New Information (Optional Step). If you cannot acquire the information you need, you will have to generate it. This is the most difficult of all of the steps. To generate information, you must acquire and enter it into your own files. The objective of performing the previous three steps is to avoid generating information that is already available in a machine-readable format.

Early studies of microcomputers showed that many users generated information that was already available in a central site. It was not uncommon for a remote location to spend hours, even hundreds of hours, generating and entering data that was already available.

There is nothing magical about the generation of new information. It involves the following time-consuming tasks:

- Locate or create the source data. This might require collecting documents and entering data from them, or doing some original effort to create data which does not currently exist.
- Enter data onto electronic media, keying or optically scanning information to get it onto machine-readable media. This task and the previous one can sometimes be performed simultaneously.
- Verify the integrity of data placed on machine-readable media. One of the challenges that every data processor must face is verifying the integrity of data entered onto computer media, to avoid using bad data. The data processing professionals have a term to describe this, GIGO, which stands for "garbage in, garbage out." Unfortunately, many novice computer users seem to think GIGO stands for "garbage in, gospel out." Users frequently do not recognize the difficulty of verifying the integrity of data entered onto machine-readable media.

At the end of these steps, one of the most time-consuming tasks will be completed. You will have the data to perform the desired processing. However, this is not a simple task. Many systems analysts believe that building up the data needed for processing consumes over half of the total data processing resources.

ACQUIRING DATA: IMPEDIMENTS AND COUNTERSTRATEGIES

Information is lifeblood of a workstation. The creation of that lifeblood might be too consuming to be practical. The solution is to find other sources of information and tap those sources. Not everyone who has information might be willing to give it away. There are three impediments that can make the acquisition of information for workstations difficult.

Impediment 1: The Turf Game. This could also be called the money game. Users create information files by entering data, verifying data, processing data, and creating and updating files using that data. This requires the user's money, blood, sweat, and tears. Therefore, the user feels he or she "owns" that data, and like many owners does not want to share these possessions with other individuals.

The solution to this impediment is to have the organization accept two premises. The first is that information is owned by the organization, and thus is not for the exclusive use of a single person. Second, information must be managed as a resource, requiring someone to be appointed manager. These concepts move data to the corporate level and make it more shareable.

Impediment 2: Ante Up. Information is not always directly transferable. It is like having the information in French when it is needed in English. At several points in the chapter the need for routines to convert data from one format to another was mentioned. These conversion routines cost time and money. Workstation users might be told that they can have the information, but they must pay for these conversion routines.

The counterstrategy to this one is simple—pay for the conversion routines. If the information is worth having, the conversion routines are worth paying for. It is not unreasonable that you, the beneficiary of an expenditure, should be charged with that expenditure.

Impediment 3: You Cannot Find What You Don't Know About. One of the major impediments to information sharing is the lack of knowledge about the existence of information. Until you know what information is available, you are not in the position to request sharing. The larger the organization, the more difficult this becomes. For example, it is not unusual for large companies to have 50,000 to 100,000 files. Although many of these files are similar, they represent slightly different versions. The challenge of identifying which among these are of value can be enormous.

The counterstrategy is to identify and document applications. Most people have neither the time nor interest to wade through thousands of computer files. A short-cut method is needed to identify the information of value. This can normally be done by first identifying the areas of business that are of interest, such as the marketing of certain product lines. This leads the user to a certain grouping of applications. The workstation user can then talk with the data processing project leaders or users responsible for those areas. Once the primary files have been identified, the workstation user can then request and study the documentation of those files to determine if some or all of that information would be of value.

SELF-ASSESSMENT CHECKLIST

You should periodically evaluate your ability to obtain and use the right data. Business opportunities might be lost for the lack of knowledge of some highly valuable data. Perhaps equally unfortunate is to spend many hours creating information which is already available in machine-readable format.

An information self-assessment checklist is provided as Fig. 7-3. This checklist is designed so that "yes" answers indicate good information prac-

	Response			
Item	Yes	No	N/A	Comments
1. Does the organization have a data dictionary?				
2. Is the information on the data dictionary used as a resource by the workstation user?				
3. Does the organization have a chief information officer, data administrator, or database administrator?				
4. Do you use one or all of the individuals available as an information resource?				
5. Does the organization have an inventory of available information?				
6. Do you use that inventory as a resource?				
7. Do you know what information is available in the organization (at least the information of interest to the workstation manager)?				
8. Do you understand the data hierarchy in the organization?				
9. Are you sufficiently skilled in reading record layouts (interpreting the meaning of data attributes)?				
10. Have you identified the types of information needed in the performance of your job?				
11. Have you investigated to determine who is the custodian of the needed data?				
12. Have you made arrangements to obtain information needed for your processing?				
13. Have you generated needed information that is not readily available from another source?				
14. Do you have the information needed to perform your job?				
15. Are routines available to download data from central sources?				
16. Are routines available to upload data from the workstation to central sources?				
17. Can data be communicated from workstation to workstation?				

Fig. 7-3. The information self-assessment checklist.

tices, and "no" answers represent potential information vulnerabilities. These items should be investigated to determine if the availability of information should be improved.

WORKSTATION RULE OF THUMB
Invariably, information obtained from central sources will be more accurate, timely, and of higher precision and integrity than that which can be generated at the local workstation.

Chapter 8

Action 6: Use the Workstation to Increase Your Productivity

Automation is recognized as the key to productivity. The workstation offers the same kind of productivity potential to the office worker as the production machine offered the factory worker. However, the productivity increase depends upon how effectively the individual manager uses the workstation.

The computer is recognized as the tool offering the greatest promise of increased productivity for the office. Although huge productivity gains at the clerical level were realized with the introduction of centralized computers, those systems have not significantly aided people at the managerial level. Many managers perform their job function in the same manner as that job was performed 50 or even 100 years ago.

The workstation is a computer that must be customized for you to best improve your productivity. However, the workstation itself will not improve productivity; only the proper use of the workstation will result in the desired productivity increase.

Productivity is an attribute of a product, referring to the rate of products produced for a given number of resources. Productivity can be increased in any of the following ways:

- Produce products with fewer resources.
- Produce more products for the same amount of resources.
- Change the products so that single products achieve the same objec-

tives that used to require several products.

• Reduce the defect rate of products so that the rework is less, which means that fewer resources have to be expended for rework.

To effectively improve your personal productivity, you need to identify the products that you produce. Because you must take specific actions to create a product at a workstation, it is sometimes easier to understand what products a manager produces in a manual environment, in which the products might be more conceptual. For example, a telephone call is a product, but might not be perceived as a product. The creation of that information placed in electronic mail, however, is clearly a product.

WHAT IS PRODUCTIVITY AND HOW IS IT MEASURED?

Productivity refers to the rate of production of products. The more products per hour, the higher the productivity. However, it is important to define the level of quality in those products, or higher productivity might mean more products of lower quality.

A product is the result of work. The products of a workstation include:

• Output reports/screens.
• Calculations.
• Analyses.
• Computer graphics.
• Creation of a file.
• Search of a file.
• Entering transactions into the workstation.
• Creation of a document (e.g., a letter or report).
• Transmission of data to another workstation, or to the central site.
• Receipt of data from another workstation, or from the central site.

The measurement of the productivity of a workstation would be in terms of one or more of these products. For example, if it took two hours to draft a letter manually, and that same letter could be created on a workstation in one hour, there was a 50 percent improvement in productivity. Productivity always refers to specific products. Therefore, until the products can be defined, it is impossible to address or measure productivity rationally.

Many managers do not view themselves as producers of products. However, this perception must change in order for you to measure your productivity increases. Companies that have productivity improvement programs find that it is difficult to convince many office managers and staff that they produce products.

A major challenge to increased productivity is the production of defect-free products. Thus, in measuring productivity it is also important to measure quality. For example, it is of little value to produce letters, reports, or analyses faster if those items are not produced correctly. Industrial psychologists have defined what they call *work-effectiveness principles*. These principles, or strategies, are what makes productivity increase. The more of these principles that can be incorporated into your job, the higher the potential for productivity. The key to productivity is using a combination of the work-effectiveness principles and systemization of work.

THE KEY TO IMPROVED PRODUCTIVITY

There are three basic managerial philosophies. One philosophy deals with control. This philosophy states that you tell people what to do, and then expect them to follow the rules precisely. The assumption is that if the process is good and they follow it, the product will be good. The problem with this philosophy is that the benefit of worker creativity and concern for good work might be lost.

The second philosophy is one of productivity. This would seem consistent with the theme of this workstation step, but it is not. An emphasis on productivity encourages people to work at their maximum speed, but this does not necessarily maximize the production of quality products. The emphasis is on producing a large number of products, not on producing quality products. It is exactly this philosophy that caused the United States to lose the lead in automotive sales.

The third philosophy places emphasis on quality. This philosophy states that it is more important to produce a quality product than to increase the speed of production. The emphasis is on assuring that all of the needed product attributes are present and correct in the final product.

Many people are surprised to find that when the emphasis is on quality, productivity will jump significantly. This occurs because when quality is emphasized, processes and standards must be developed to ensure that the desired attributes are present in the finished product. This is referred to by those responsible for product quality as *quality control*. Having defined what is wanted, and with processes built to ensure those attributes will be present in the final product, productivity jumps significantly. This experience has occurred over and over again in the organizations that emphasize quality. Thus, in the quest for improving personal productivity, there must be a quest for quality. With that quest must go a systematic process subject to quality control measures. It is the systematic process that increases your personal productivity.

To translate this philosophy on quality into your everyday work at the workstation, the principle that you must incorporate is quality of work. Initially, you must forget speed of work and concentrate on quality. In previous chapters you have been asked to perform tasks which are quality-oriented, such as developing procedures—these are important in controlling the quality of the workstation product. Emphasis on reliability of data is another quality characteristic.

The argument against doing these tasks is that they take too much time.

However, you must accept the fact that in the beginning it will take you much longer to do tasks on the workstation, and concentrate on performing the actions that will permit you to produce quality products, such as developing procedures. The speed and productivity gains that you hope to accomplish will occur in a few weeks. On the other hand, if you push to get work through the workstation and disregard the quality principles, you might find that the frustrations associated with unwanted problems cause you to abandon the workstation.

WORKSTATION RULE OF THUMB
Productivity is worthless without quality. Quality must be the cornerstone on which productivity is based.

PRODUCTIVITY IMPROVEMENT STRATEGIES

The strategies that you should use to improve your personal productivity are the actions outlined in this book, together with the principles of work-effectiveness. These principles create job functions that are conducive to productivity increases. They can be used to design workstation tasks that improve personal productivity.

One of the challenges facing many managers is the value of the products being produced. Work-effectiveness principles not only address motivation to produce, but address the value and importance of the product. Productivity increases are not limited to producing products faster, but can also occur from eliminating the creation of unneeded or unimportant products. Also, the implementation of these principles will cause you to rethink who should produce the products. You might identify products that can be better produced by lower-level workers.

Installing a workstation will cause a significant restructuring of your job. Use this as an opportunity to rethink your job tasks. You should analyze your current job to determine if it is properly structured, if the tasks are necessary, if they need to be done by you, and if not, ensure that the restructuring for the workstation incorporates the appropriate changes. This restructuring might also increase your subordinates' productivity, as well as increasing your own productivity. The recommended personal productivity improvement strategies are listed in Fig. 8-1.

Strategy 1: Download Jobs to the Lowest Organizational Level that can Perform the Job. The concept of downloading means that tasks are moved down the organizational structure to the lowest point at which they can be effectively executed. Practice shows that many tasks are performed at the wrong organizational level. If the wrong person is assigned a job, it can cause problems. Let's look at an actual example.

In the mid-1960s the initial emphasis on computer security occurred. One of the proposed solutions that had general acceptance worldwide was to have

Number	Strategy	Description
1.	Downloading	Shifting responsibilities and tasks to the lowest organizational level (person) which can perform that task.
2.	Skill combination	Structuring tasks to include as many skills as possible.
3.	Task importance	Emphasizing to the individual performing the task the importance of that task to the business.
4.	Feedback	Providing information on the performance of a task to enable the task performer to evaluate performance.
5.	Social interaction	Building into a job an interface with people involved or related to the performance of a task.

Fig. 8-1. Personal productivity improvement strategies.

operators challenge the authority of an individual to be present in the computer room. This solution quickly failed, because operators did not perceive it appropriate to challenge the rights of members of senior management, auditors, or other important individuals to be present in the computer room. Over time, the concept was recognized to be incorrectly placed in the organization, and the responsibility was transferred to the computer room supervisor.

Although this example illustrates the uploading of responsibility, downloading is the normal result of rethinking who should perform a task. It is much more common for tasks to be performed at too high a level than at too low a level.

When determining how to best utilize your workstation, you should put great emphasis on the downloading principle. Two types of downloading can occur. One is the downloading of those managerial tasks that are best performed by subordinates. The second is downloading tasks to the workstation. For example, should you perform an analysis, or can it best be done by workstation capabilities? Analyze your tasks to determine whether or not the performance of a task is an effective use of your time. If it is not, then you should determine whether part or all of that task can be performed by the workstation, or by a subordinate.

The result of this downloading exercise will be a reshuffling of job responsibilities. The result will be that you will be performing only those job tasks that you cannot delegate to subordinates. This will give you more free time to do the managerial functions of organizing, planning, directing, and controlling.

The downloading exercise is one that snowballs productivity. The first wave effect is the unloading of inappropriately assigned or very time-consuming responsibilities. This extra time can be used in determining better ways to do work which produces the second wave of productivity. This is productivity improvement through better methods.

Downloading to subordinates produces the third wave of productivity. Providing subordinates with more rewarding work increases their motivation, and thus increases their productivity. It also encourages subordinates to download their work to lower levels (if practical), and the productivity snowball rolls on.

Strategy 2: Combine as Many Skills Into a Single Job Task as Possible. Productivity is closely tied to motivation. Tasks which only require a single skill are less motivating, causing productivity to decrease. For example, if you have to spend eight hours performing straightforward financial analysis, only your computing skill might be needed. This can result in your becoming bored, which in turn reduces your productivity. The lack of attention to detail will increase your rate of errors.

Jobs should incorporate as many skills as practical. Each task should be examined to identify the number of skills incorporated into the task. If the number of skills is very low, the probability of increasing productivity significantly is also low. It might also mean the task should not be performed by you.

In the manufacture of the Volvo automobile, management wanted to improve worker productivity and reduce the number of defects that were occurring. At the time this objective was established, the Volvo production line was one comprised of specialists. Each did a highly specialized task, but unfortunately that task only required a single skill. The workers became bored, and it affected both their productivity and quality of work. Volvo management changed the concept to incorporate the use of multiple skills into a single job. For example, teams were created with responsibility for building and troubleshooting an entire engine, rather than limiting the responsibility of the worker to installing a single component of the engine. The result was both significantly increased productivity, and the production of higher quality engines.

You need to apply this principle to your workstation processing by building jobs that incorporate multiple skills. For example, don't create a long, time-consuming task that just involves entering data into the computer. Consider restructuring that task so you might enter a small amount of data, do some processing, do some personal analysis, get some output, and then go on to enter more data. This approach makes the job more interesting, and thus will help increase job productivity.

The practice of task combination requires work to be systemized in a manner that facilitates work flow. Software packages that have included this principle are proving to be much more valuable than software packages that are single-skill oriented. For example, VisiCalc dominated the spreadsheet market when it was first introduced. However, it was a single-skill package. Lotus 1-2-3 combined the spreadsheet skill with graphics and file maintenance, which resulted in an increase in productivity due to the concept of task and skill combination.

Strategy 3: People Work Harder On Tasks They Think Are Important. The importance of a task relates to both its actual and perceived importance. If it is important to the organization but unimportant to the individual, it is a potential productivity problem. On the other hand, if it is important to the individual but not important to the organization, it might result in an ineffective use of resources. People are more productive doing work that they think is important. If the work is perceived as "busy work," the individual has difficulty becoming motivated to do the work either well or fast. To put this principle into practice, the management of a company should contribute to the employees' perception of the importance of tasks. This can be done by telling your subordinates how important their work is to the company.

The work tasks will vary according to the position the individual has. Thus, the importance of a task might also vary by who is viewing that task. What might be considered important to a clerk might not be important to a senior manager, and vice versa. All that is necessary for this principle to work is for the person doing the job to believe that the job task is important.

The key, then, between task importance and productivity is one of demonstrating the importance of the task. From a managerial perspective, this should not be difficult. What might be difficult is to cull out the unimportant tasks, so that they can either be downloaded or combined with other relatively unimportant tasks, the sum of which becomes important.

It is necessary in defining tasks to define the level of importance of those tasks. The importance must then be related to the individual who will do the tasks. If you end up with tasks that appear to have minimal importance, those tasks should be transferred to workstation processing wherever possible. It is highly probable that the manager can at least semi-automate many of the less important tasks on a workstation, if they cannot be transferred to subordinates.

Strategy 4: Know How Well You Are Doing. *Feedback* is an integral part of any productivity program. Unless people know how they are doing, it is difficult for them to evaluate their performance. If you cannot evaluate your own performance, you will also not be able to determine the number or quality of the products produced.

Feedback can be both automated and manual. Automated feedback is preferable. People are much more receptive to feedback provided by machines than feedback provided by people. This phenomenon occurs because the automated feedback is consistent, based on predetermined rules, and is unemotional. Feedback provided by people might be based on arbitrary rules and frequently is presented in a manner which might be offensive.

When you do work on the workstation, you will receive a lot of feedback. Each action you do normally gets a programmed response from the workstation. Some level of feedback is already incorporated into the system, other types of feedback must be added. The type of feedback needed will be dependent upon the workstation objectives. These must be clearly established, and then feedback mechanisms introduced to determine whether or not those objectives have been accomplished. Some feedback mechanisms will be relatively easy to add if, for example, the feedback involves statistical information collected during operation, such as the number of transactions processed. Other types might be difficult to get.

The type of feedback information that is readily available in most workstation processing includes notification that:

- Incorrect values were entered into processing.
- Unidentifiable instructions were used.
- Incorrect commands were used.
- Data overflow conditions occurred, for example, too many items entered into a table or spreadsheet.
- System rules were violated, for example, an event was performed in the wrong sequence.
- System control identified a problem, for example, financial entries do not balance.
- Processing is incomplete, for example, you failed to enter all of the data needed for processing.

This feedback information is indicative of the ability or inability to do the process right the first time. The occurrence of these conditions represents a potential productivity loss. However, the identification, quantification, and action taken on defects will have the long-term benefit of improving productivity. If the defects are not appropriately noted and recorded, the same type of error will be repeated day after day, with the associated continual loss of productivity. Most commercial workstation software does not collect data on the number of user errors. If you want that information, you will probably have to develop the process to collect and analyze it.

Strategy 5: Encourage Social Interaction. Productivity is improved as individuals interact with each other. This occurs because a task can be viewed from a much larger perspective. For example, if programmers are allowed to interact with users, operators, and database administrators, they can better visualize the relationship between what they are doing and the totality of the job in which they are involved. If people are excluded from this social interface, their view of work becomes much narrower, and their productivity decreases.

In the workstation environment, social interaction can be through other workstations or other facilities. This principle applied to workstation processing means that workstations must be connected in networks. An individual working alone will not be as productive as that individual linked with other workstations and the information and intelligence available through those workstations.

Social interaction can be also be interpreted to be information interaction. In other words, linking workstations to other data bases and sources of information is a productivity tool. The wider the range of activities and information a workstation is coupled with, the higher the productivity of that individual.

How to Use Work-Effectiveness Principles

The five work-effectiveness principles are included in this book for two purposes. First, if other people are designing your workstation capabilities and recommending how you use those capabilities, you can challenge them with work-effectiveness principles. For example, if they are developing tasks for you that are single-skill tasks, break you social link with other individuals, or provide minimal feedback, you can anticipate that these new workstation tasks will not be personally rewarding. This might have a negative impact on your personal productivity. Second, you can use the principles to better construct your job and those of your subordinates.

Some managers are reluctant to use workstations because they believe it is more of a clerical function than a management function. Thus, the workstation is not viewed as important. Importance is a work-effectiveness principle. Therefore, if managers do not think workstations are important, they will not want to utilize workstations in their jobs.

Through the study of these principles you should begin to understand how the workstation utilizes many of the workstation principles. These principles should help you understand how the workstation can improve your work-effectiveness. Thus, not only do these principles provide you with the information that you need to properly construct your job, but they provide you with the basis for analyzing how the workstation will impact your job, and the value of that impact.

WORKSTATION RULE OF THUMB
Use the work-effectiveness principles to determine whether the workstation will increase your job effectiveness or decrease it. If it increases, use the workstation; if effectiveness is decreased, avoid using the workstation.

ACHIEVING PERSONAL PRODUCTIVITY IMPROVEMENTS

Productivity is improved through the introduction of systems. Rarely can an artist improve his/her productivity unless the artistic endeavor can be reduced to a process. Artists who want to produce a large number of products develop systems for producing them. Once the system has been established, it can then be improved, which in turn should improve productivity.

Managers operating workstations can rarely improve their personal productivity until they develop a system for performing their work. Even if the system does not show an immediate jump in productivity, it provides the base on which productivity improvements can be built. A four-step process to achieve personal productivity improvements is listed in Fig. 8-2.

The developers of workstation applications should define the procedures you are to follow in doing work. In some cases, these systems are well thought-

Number	Step	Description	Responsibilities
1.	Establish systems for workstation operation.	Develop step-by-step procedures that provide a standardized method for performing a task (downloading, skill combination, task importance, feedback, social interaction).	○ System designer ○ Workstation user
2.	Set workstation processing objectives and measure results.	Measurable objectives should be established as a basis for measuring performance.	○ Workstation user
3.	Identify and count processing defects.	Errors and unwanted results from workstation performance should be categorized and counted.	○ Workstation user
4.	Modify workstation systems to meet processing objectives and reduce defects.	Processes should be continually improved by making changes to reduce high-frequency problems (downloading, skill combination, task importance, feedback, social interaction).	○ Workstation user

Fig. 8-2. Achieving personal productivity improvements.

out and defined; in other instances, a task is stated as a series of unrelated instructions on how the different capabilities operate. In some instances, the system deals exclusively with the automated part of the task; in other instances, it contains all of the procedures from when you start a job through its completion.

A system is a process for completing work. Just as this chapter is outlining a system for improving productivity, so should workstation systems be established as a step-by-step process. The objective of a system is to provide a method that enables two people performing the same task using the same system to produce exactly the same results.

After the system has been established, usage objectives can be established. These usage objectives should be described in measurable terms, and then measured to determine whether or not they are achieved. For example, a simple objective might be to reduce the time of performing a given task from six hours to two hours. Another objective could be to reduce the number of defects or errors in the process from four to one.

Objectives and measurement are only realistic after a system has been established. It is generally impractical to measure an unstructured task, because the exact task might not be able to be reproduced a second time, or by another individual. Therefore, the measurement would not be indicative of what can be accomplished the next time.

A *defect* is a variance between what should have happened and what actually occurred—an unexpected result of any type. It can be something that should have been done but was not done, something that was done incorrectly, or something that was done that was not required to be done. The identification and counting of defects involves the following three tasks.

Task 1: A scheme for categorizing defects must be developed. Rarely do workstations provide this capability. Although it is difficult to generalize a defect scheme, because of the variety of uses of workstations, defects include the following:

- Data entry errors.
- Misinterpretation of processing rules.
- Misinterpretation of application rules.
- Incorrect sequence in processing.
- Incorrect response to error messages.
- Incorrect interpretation of output.
- Failure to enter an appropriate parameter.
- Hardware failure.
- Software failure.
- Incorrect data downloaded from, or uploaded to, another system.

Task 2: Record the defects experienced. In most workstation systems, this currently must be done manually. This task would require the user to develop a small log and keep a record as defects occur. If this log is kept near the workstation, it will not take much effort to complete.

Task 3: Quantify and summarize the occurrence of defects. These problems can then be discussed with the developers of the systems and workstation processes. A high frequency of the same type of error should be addressed and solution determined to reduce the frequency of that type of defect.

You might be questioning the need to perform some of these steps. A logical question would be "Isn't there an easier way?" Unfortunately, when you work with highly complex and sophisticated systems, such as workstations, the careful recording of defects and attention to detail pays off. It is similar to building a complex model. If you don't pay close attention to putting the first pieces together, you might find that near the end of the building process you have a real mess.

Productivity improvement occurs through a *bootstrapping* process. The bootstrapping process can only begin when a system is established. You identify the problems in the system, and then you eliminate the cause of the problems. Utilizing this bootstrapping process, the productivity will continually increase through continual self-assessment. The bootstrapping method should identify the more significant defects first. Failure to meet performance objectives because of a high rate of defects should be promptly addressed. The identification and accumulation of defects permits the high-frequency defects to be identified and acted upon.

Whenever the system is changed, the defects measurement process should be emphasized. If the change was designed to eliminate a problem, measurement will tell whether the change was effective. If not, the system should be restored to the original version and another change made. This process continues until the problem is eliminated. At this point, the next defect is attacked, and so on.

PERSONAL PRODUCTIVITY IMPROVEMENT: IMPEDIMENTS AND COUNTERSTRATEGIES

Productivity improvement is not always a major priority for everybody. This is especially true when working with a new technology. You might be totally involved in just mastering the technology, so that completing a job seems sufficiently rewarding, without worrying about productivity.

Productivity should only become a goal after the technology is mastered. Learn to do the job right first. When performance appears unproductive, there is a tendency to cease workstation operations, or to rely less upon this new tool. That is why a plan to increase productivity is so important. As productivity increases, you tend to rely more and more upon workstation processing.

Several impediments affect a manager's workstation productivity. The first impediment is that most people believe that hard work will produce more good products per unit of time. However, experience has shown that hard work might help productivity, but it is not the key to productivity. Problem-free processes enable productivity gains to occur.

You must be convinced that an emphasis on quality and predefined systems procedures is the key to productivity, in order to make that productivity happen. This concept must be experienced before it can be believed. People teaching quality and productivity concepts prefer to demonstrate that the principles work, rather than explain them. After you become a believer in the quality and productivity concepts, the principles are quickly implemented, and your productivity increases.

The second impediment is caused by an improper reward system. People respond to rewards. Rewards are the basis for changing behavior. Therefore, when you go from an unproductive process to a productive process, there should be a reward associated with that change in behavior. This reward need not be monetary. It can be the reward of doing a better job. However, without a reward, there might be insufficient incentive to encourage an individual to push for increased productivity.

The sole counterstrategy to this impediment is to change the reward system. If senior management wants productivity increases, it must give rewards for those productivity gains. If the reward is given for factors other than productivity, then people will do whatever is rewarded. Although you might not be able to change the rewards your supervisor gives you, you can at least practice and promote the concept with your subordinates.

The third impediment deals with productivity improvements that cannot be measured. Positive evidence of productivity increases must be provided by predefined measurement processes. People thinking or hoping that they have done well is not good enough. The actual change in productivity must be measured in terms that are readily understandable. Without measurements, there is uncertainty, and with uncertainty there is a loss of motivation. You need to know how much the workstation helps you in your job.

The method to overcome this impediment is to put productivity measurements in place. Clearly establishing productivity objectives, and then measuring your workstation execution against those objectives, demonstrates whether or not productivity has been increased.

SELF-ASSESSMENT CHECKLIST

Productivity increases are calculated by measuring performance changes over a period of time. As productivity measurements become more quantitative, the rate of change of production can be more specifically stated. The self-assessment exercise that follows is an evaluation of the process which permits productivity to be increased. It does not measure specific productivity gains but, rather, the effectiveness of the processes that encourage productivity gains.

The productivity self-assessment checklist is provided in Fig. 8-3. This questionnaire evaluates a number of items related to your company's productivity improvement program. "Yes" responses indicate positive aspects of such

	Response			
Item	Yes	No	N/A	Comments
1. Is producing quality products the primary objective of the organization?				
2. Have productivity objectives been established?				
3. Have the involved individuals participated in setting the productivity objectives?				
4. Have work-effectiveness principles been included in programs to improve productivity?				
5. Are tasks downloaded to the lowest possible skill level to perform those tasks?				
6. Wherever appropriate, have tasks been arranged so that they involve multiple skills?				
7. Has the importance of each task been emphasized to the individual performing the task?				
8. Have feedback mechanisms been established for each task so the individual performing that task can assess his/her performance?				
9. Is the feedback information quantitative?				
10. Do the job tasks include interaction with the other people involved in the success of that task?				
11. Are the organization's reward systems tied to increases in productivity?				
12. Is it a workstation objective to establish systems and methods for performing workstation tasks?				
13. Have the various types of workstation defects been identified?				
14. Has a scheme been established for categorizing workstation defects?				
15. Has a process been established for recording workstation defects?				
16. Has a process been established for quantifying and reporting workstation defects?				
17. Have the defects been prioritized in order of importance?				
18. Is the process changed to reduce the high-priority defects?				

Fig. 8-3. The personal productivity self-assessment checklist.

a program, while "no" responses represent potential impediments to improving productivity. Such items should be investigated to determine their impact on a productivity improvement program.

WORKSTATION RULE OF THUMB
Productivity as a goal is worthless without an emphasis on quality. Producing more bad products per hour should not be the objective. The objective should be to produce more quality products per hour.

Chapter 9

Action 7: Build Communication Interfaces

Communication interfaces will never replace face-to-face interfaces. On the other hand, workstation communications can be a more efficient means of communication information than interoffice correspondence, widespread distributions, and playing "telephone tag" with hard-to-find colleagues.

More and more of management's *interface*—communication with others—will be through electronic media. This chapter addresses the types and construction of electronic interfaces for communications. The emphasis is on internal communication, but the external electronic communication with customers, suppliers, and business colleagues is also addressed.

Someone once said that the only thing constant is change. The way business was conducted in the 1930s is different than the 1950s, which is different from the 1980s. Most likely, the methods of doing business in the 1990s will change to keep pace with technology changes.

ADVANTAGES AND DISADVANTAGES
OF ELECTRONIC COMMUNICATION

The move to electronic interfaces between managers is a tidal wave that cannot be stopped. It needs to be understood, and your means of performing your communication tasks adjusted accordingly. This section is not designed to help you decide whether or not to use electronic interfaces but, rather, to help you adapt to them.

The advantages of electronic interfacing are overwhelming. An understanding of these advantages will encourage you to use this new capability. Change is always easier when you are convinced it is to your advantage to make the change. The five main advantages to electronic interfacing are:

1: Increased speed of communication. Electronic messages move faster than manually carried messages. Electronic systems move communications more quickly between people or groups of people. For example, many people can receive the same information almost simultaneously using electronic interfacing. As soon as information is available, those with a need to know can know it.

2: Increased interchange between people. Electronic systems can transmit data to large numbers of people with great ease. Communication also becomes simpler, because there are fewer administrative tasks to perform, such as preparing envelopes and duplicating information on paper. The ease with which communications can occur facilitates an increase of communication between people.

3: Less time spent in meetings. Information that previously needed to be transferred at a meeting can now be transferred electronically. For example, previously, when you wanted a group of individuals to be aware of a situation, a meeting might have to be called for that purpose. Now that information can be transmitted electronically without the time spent at a meeting.

4: Reduced personal travel time. Managers spend a large amount of time traveling to meetings and distributing information to other people. If this information can be sent electronically, the time spent by the manager in traveling is saved.

5: Direct transmission to recipient. Electronic transmission sends the communication directly to the recipient. There are no intermediate parties involved, with a possibility that the communication will not be delivered, or be delayed en route.

The disadvantage of electronic communication is primarily the loss of face-to-face contact with other people. There is a communication and rapport that occurs in this face-to-face communication which is lost in electronic interfacing. This disadvantage is controllable by selecting the communication alternative best suited for the purpose. Electronic interfacing provides another means, but is not meant to fully replace face-to-face communication.

The main disadvantages to electronic interfacing are:

1: Less personal communication. Electronic messages are normally formal and to the point. The type of greetings and salutations that would be associated with a face-to-face meeting, or telephone conversation, are normally left out of electronic interfacing.

2: Greater probability of misunderstanding. Electronic interfacing tends to replace one-to-one communication. With face-to-face or voice-to-voice communication, there is the opportunity to clarify and explain misunderstood facts or concepts. With electronic communication, such questioning and probing might not occur. A misunderstood piece of information might stay misunderstood.

3: Lack of assurance that the message is received. Communications sent electronically are gone when transmitted. In many instances, there is no positive feedback that the recipient actually received the information. Therefore, while the sender believes the recipient knows the information, the recipient might not have received it, or might not have inquired about messages waiting to be received.

Electronic interfacing is a new phenomenon to most managers. They are familiar with telegrams and other electronic communication, but have not had the personal capability to generate and transmit communication before the acquisition of their own workstation. It is important that these managers understand not only how electronic communication functions, but also what concerns they should have about the proper use of these new communication tools.

AVAILABILITY OF COMMUNICATION CAPABILITIES

Companies are moving into the electronic communication age at varying speeds. Some large corporations are contemplating the use of satellites to facilitate communication among their employees worldwide. Some organizations have telephone numbers that will tie an individual into the internal electronic communication system. With this capability, any touch-tone telephone in the world becomes a direct link to any workstation or employee within the organization. Other organizations have yet to install the new communication capabilities. Sometimes the advantages are not understood, or the company lacks the in-house expertise to develop and install the new methods. The skills required to develop and implement these new systems is different than the skills needed for many current computer systems.

Today's electronic interface systems are the first generation of a new wave of communication possibilities. The capabilities on the drawing boards propose significant extensions to today's capabilities. Low-cost telephones with video screens will address some of the loss of personal amenities. Portable communication devices will be used to communicate directly with key individuals, wherever they are. Ease of transmitting documents and graphics will improve understanding.

Electronic communication and interfacing will become a more important aspect of business. Companies that do not communicate electronically will be at a disadvantage in the marketplace. Many people believe that the implementation of these new technologies is essential for survival in tomorrow's business world.

ELECTRONIC INTERFACE STRATEGIES

Most of the electronic interface strategies are beyond the scope of the individual workstation user. The user is more involved in deciding whether or not to use communication capabilities, not creating those capabilities. Establishing communication networks and developing the supporting hardware and software is a technically complex task.

Workstation users can lobby for new facilities. Capabilities which have not been implemented yet, but could be implemented, might be considered because of your interest in them. You need to understand what could be available, and then make judgments regarding the need for those capabilities.

The uses for electronic communication interfaces are listed in Fig. 9-1 and described below.

Electronic Mail. This is currently the most popular form of electronic interfacing. Electronic mail provides the opportunity for an individual to send a message to another. The electronic mail system must include an addressing system to permit easy identification of the addressee.

Electronic Filing Cabinet. This capability provides for the storage and retrieval of electronic information. It can be used to contain lists of information, such as addresses, electronic documents, messages sent in electronic mail, or files of reference information. Some people use their workstation to identify where, in a physical filing cabinet, they have stored a document.

Electronic In-Basket. This capability is normally associated with electronic mail. It provides a repository for messages and mail to be held until the recipient calls for those messages. Some systems have a limit on the size of the electronic in-basket, while others provide almost unlimited storage capacity. Some advanced systems permit an electronic voice to read the messages to a recipient when a workstation or other device with a display screen is not available. This enables people who are traveling or at home to collect information awaiting them in the electronic in-basket.

Electronic Mail Memo. This is a variation of electronic mail, in which longer memos can be transmitted to many people. The mail memos usually involve distribution lists. For example, if the personnel department wants to alert all managers to a new personnel procedure, they could develop and transmit that memo to all managers on the personnel manager list. Memos tend to be less personal than official documents of the organization or of a section within the organization.

Number	Strategy	Description
1.	Electronic mail	Transmission of messages in printed format from workstation to workstation.
2.	Electronic filing cabinet	Storage of information in a readily retrievable form to the workstation.
3.	Electronic in-basket	Holding information in the storage area until called for by the workstation user.
4.	Electronic mail memo	Transmission of documents to one or more users, normally based on a distribution list.
5.	Electronic decisions	Use of workstations as a vehicle to comment on and/or approved managerial actions.
6.	Electronic conferencing	Electronic dialog, normally through message transmission, between two or more workstations.
7.	Electronic bulletin board	Storage of common information that can be scanned in request.
8.	Electronic upload/download	Movement of data from workstations to central facilities, or central facilities down to workstations.
9.	Electronic external communication	Electronic communication with individuals or facilities at sites outside the organization.
10.	Electronic telephone book and dialing	Quick retrieval of telephone numbers and an automatic dialing facility to connect with those numbers.

Fig. 9-1. Uses of electronic interfaces.

Electronic Decisions. Electronic decisions are one of the least used strategies, but one that has great potential. The system is already in place in most federal and state legislatures. It provides the opportunity for legislators to vote electronically, and for the results to be recorded electronically. Although this is a very formal use of electronic decision-making, less formal uses offer greater potential in business organizations.

Electronic decisions could be made on policies, procedures, and standards. The information could be transmitted to the involved parties for their immediate feedback. In some instances, decision-making merely means the opportunity to react and comment, not necessarily voting.

Electronic decision-making is very consistent with a research technique called the Delphi Technique. This is a problem-solving technique in which the parties involved have the opportunity to react on documents, such as procedures and standards. In electronic decision-making, the parties involved will have the opportunity to see the reaction and comment of the other parties. This allows each decision-maker the opportunity to react, and all other decision-makers have the opportunity to see that reaction and change their comments accordingly. For some documents, this form of decision-making might be far superior to a group sitting around a table at a meeting. It forces comments to be reduced to writing for analysis and reaction.

The concept also permits a manager to question subordinates quickly regarding a local managerial decision. Again, these decision opportunities need not be a voting situation but, rather, a polling of the reactions of the involved parties. Without electronic decision-making, the scheduling and time involved in a meeting might be prohibitive. Electronic decision-making can involve a large number of people with a minimum expenditure of time.

Electronic Conferencing. This is best accomplished with a video supplement and an electronic blackboard. Current workstation facilities limit this strategy to an elementary conferencing approach. However, a small group of people can interact in a conferencing mode through keyboard communication if only minimal information needs are addressed.

Electronic Bulletin Boards. This process enables anyone to post information that might be of interest to others on a specific topic. For example, there might be a bulletin board on potential workstation problems. If a workstation user encounters a problem, that problem is posted to the electronic bulletin board to be scanned by any other workstation user. Normally, the length of time that a message can appear on the bulletin board is limited.

Electronic Upload/Download. This concept of transmitting large amounts of data to and from different workstation sites or central computers was introduced in Chapter 7. It is one of the most valuable uses of electronic interfacing, because the network can provide higher speed transmission of files with fewer errors.

Electronic External Communication. This is a general category of capabilities. It normally requires communication between individuals over common carrier (telephone company) communication lines. Some arrangements must be made in the organization's communication system before this capability exists. Some common carriers already provide the capability to permit this type of external electronic communication to occur through their facilities.

While not used extensively yet, it promises to be one of the more powerful means of conducting business between organizations.

Electronic Telephone Book and Dialing. This capability couples the telephone with the workstation. It adds a workstation capability that permits an individual telephone number to be located electronically, and then dialed automatically. This system can be designed to redial within a specified period of time if the line is busy or there is no answer.

These current interface strategies are the beginning of a communication revolution. Not only will more capabilities be added, but the capabilities will be combined in a way that will make the new capability more powerful than the sum of the individual capabilities.

BUILDING ELECTRONIC INTERFACES

Moving from one form of conducting business to another is a significant change in the way a manager performs works. Someone who has used telephone and paper communication might find it difficult to switch to electronic communication through a workstation. For some managers, the change will mean generating a message and transmitting it themselves, instead of delegating the task to others.

Do not equate the task of manually preparing a letter or report to the process of doing the same function on a workstation. For example, when you manually prepare a message, you must indicate the list of recipients. You might also need to indicate their location, title, and address. With an electronic workstation, you can develop a list of recipients, and then use it to send a message to everyone on the list. If you wanted to send a memo to all of your sales managers, and that was List A, all you would need to indicate is that the following message goes to everyone on List A, and they would all receive it. In addition, parts of the message might already be in storage. For example, certain paragraphs or parts of the message can come from other processes you have performed, such as spreadsheet processing. In the manual preparation of a message, you might have to reference several documents, and dictate or write the entire message. With an electronic workstation, a few powerful commands could generate most of the message quickly.

The major challenge in using electronic interfaces is understanding the new capabilities, and then using them effectively. This process can best be done by first understanding what is being done now, and then determining how that can be adapted to the new methods. Planning is always preferable, rather than waiting for the appropriate situation to occur to use the new electronic means.

A four-step process for implementing an electronic communication capability into your job function is illustrated in Fig. 9-2. This methodology does not establish the electronic network but, rather, puts into place the procedures for using that network.

Step 1: Establish an Interface/Communication Baseline. An *interface/communication baseline* is a profile of the types of communication now being conducted by the manager. The objective of this baseline is to identify communication tasks to handle through electronic interfaces. You cannot fully comprehend the potential value of electronic interfacing until a baseline has been established.

The baseline should include all current repetitive communications. The recommended period for accumulating the baseline is one week. Although there are special communications that occur less frequently than weekly, all high-volume communications normally occur within a one-week period. Adding the monthly, quarterly, and annual communications normally does not add a significant workload, and in many instances the less frequent communication is highly specialized, as with budgets.

A form for recording current communications is provided as Fig. 9-3. This worksheet is designed to record nonelectronic communications. For a one-week period, you should record the following information on the form:

- A unique number, beginning with 1 and continuing sequentially.
- A short description of each communication. It is not necessary to list every communication, but, rather, categories of communication. For ex-

Number	Step	Description	Responsibilities
1.	Establish an interface/communication baseline.	Develop a log of the type of communications currently being conducted.	○ Workstation user
2.	Identify electronic interface/communication alternatives.	For each of the communication items on the baseline log, identify electronic alternatives.	○ Workstation user ○ System developer
3.	Select and learn alternative means of interface/communication.	Take action to utilize the electronic alternative where the benefits appear to warrant the change in communication methods.	○ Workstation user
4.	Use electronic interface/communication network.	Connect into a network that permits the electronic alternate methods to become operational.	○ Workstation developers ○ Workstation user

Fig. 9-2. Building electronic interfaces.

Number	Communication	Frequency	Volume	Party	Method	Electronic Alternative

Fig. 9-3. The interface/communication baseline worksheet.

ample, telephone calls might be divided into three or four categories for purposes of establishing a baseline. However, all communications should be included, including one-to-one meetings, group meetings, correspondence, etc.

• The number of times within a week that a certain type of communication occurs.

• The volume, expressed in either number of words, for written communication, or time, for verbal communication. Verbal communication can be translated to about 300 words per minute.

• The individual or individuals involved in the communication. If it is appropriate, specific names or titles can be used, if not, the number of parties involved should be sufficient.

• The means by which the communication occurred. For example, letter, telephone call, memo, formal meeting, or informal meeting.

Each communication should be recorded on the worksheet during the baseline week. At the end of one week, the worksheet task will have been completed. After the recording is completed, you should categorize and summarize the communication by type. For example, if there are many communications of the same type, they might be combined at the end of the week, such as late payment notices to customers. If you know that certain types of communications will be occurring frequently, such as memos to your staff, a single worksheet can be devoted to that staff communication, so that at the end of the week, it can be easily categorized.

Step 2: Identify Electronic Interface/Communication Alternatives. The communication capabilities available with workstations should be considered as alternatives for the communications method documented on the baseline worksheet. This involves understanding what alternative electronic means are available to you, and then determining if an alternative is suitable for the type of communication being undertaken. The objective of this step is to identify communication tasks to incorporate into workstation processing.

It is normally helpful to conduct this step with someone who understands the communication capabilities of the workstation. The baseline worksheets and the capabilities from Fig. 9-1 provide the basis for that communication. If an alternative method is available and appears appropriate, it should be recorded on the baseline worksheet in the column for electronic alternatives. In some instances, there might be more than one alternative to satisfy specific communication needs. This should also be indicated.

Step 3: Select and Learn the Electronic Alternative of Interface/Communication. The decision on how to conduct the communication resides with you. The considerations will not only involve the electronic alternatives, but the cost of those alternatives, the availability of individuals you communicate with in the communication network, and the amount of effort required to communicate electronically compared with the current method. All of these considerations must be included in your decision-making process.

If an alternative method is selected, you must learn how to operate that alternative method. This might involve formal training, or one of the other training alternatives discussed in Chapter 4. It is important for you to master the new method, so you feel confident about using the new capability before you actually begin using that capability in your day-to-day work.

Step 4: Use Electronic Interface/Communication Network. Workstations might be connected into communication networks. If your workstation is connected to a communication network, the other workstations or facilities with which you can communicate might be limited. For example, your network might only permit you to access the central computer site. A request on your part might be necessary to ensure that you are connected with all those individuals with whom you communicate. This might require you to have the capability of entering the telephone network, so that you can communicate with individuals outside of your company.

In most companies, there is an individual who is responsible for the communication network. It might be necessary to have the approval of that individual to enter the network. In addition, there might be charges for using the network system, which will require the establishment of a budget, accounts, or other means of charging the cost of the facility to the user.

The result of performing these four steps will be entry into, and use of, a communication network. The methodology just described is designed to prepare you to use the communication facility. At this point, you are ready to begin actually using the network as a means of communication.

ELECTRONIC INTERFACE: IMPEDIMENTS AND COUNTERSTRATEGIES

It has proved extremely difficult in many organizations to get managers to use electronic communications. This is particularly true of established managers who have developed very effective communication networks. These networks are based on years of interfacing and building mutual trust between individuals. The concern of these managers is that the electronic methods will not be as effective as the current proven communication systems.

There are three major impediments that must be addressed. The first involves lack of feedback. Telephone and personal communication provide instant feedback. This does not mean that there are no problems in this type of communication, just that the opportunity to clarify situations is improved through the immediate feedback of comments. In electronic communication, there might be no feedback, delayed feedback, or feedback that is difficult to interpret.

The counterstrategy is to build feedback mechanisms into electronic communication. One of the most important feedback mechanisms is notification that a specific communication has been received. This acknowledgement can be expanded to indicate agreement or disagreement, acceptance or rejection. Other procedures can be developed to provide more sophisticated feedback, if necessary.

The second impediment involves loss of personal contact. Many managers are reluctant to use electronic communication, because of the potential loss of a network of contact and colleagues. This contact and trust is built up over a period of time through numerous personal interactions. The lack of this contact is perceived to affect the relationships that they have with other people. Also, if a message or communication draws a strong negative response, the individual does not have the opportunity to observe and react immediately to that negative response.

The counterstrategy is to select the most appropriate communication means. Electronic communication should be viewed as an alternative, not a replacement, to current communication networks. It provides the option to select the most effective communication means, based on the information being communicated. You might seriously evaluate when and why the electronic communication networks are superior to personal, face-to-face communication.

The third impediment is an unwillingness to change. Some managers just do not like change. This is not a unique trait to managers. The effort required to learn a new system might seem overwhelming. In addition, many managers are successful using the current mode of communication, and might be unsuccessful using the new mode. Thus, it appears to be a situation in which an individual can only lose, not win.

The counterstrategy is to introduce new concepts slowly. Managers must become convinced that electronic communications will make them more successful. This is normally best accomplished by introducing the concepts on a limited basis. For example, electronic mail can help address the challenge of "telephone tag." When they see the benefit of this, the other uses might make more sense. The slow introduction of a new concept helps build confidence in the benefits to be derived from new technology.

SELF-ASSESSMENT CHECKLIST

The use of electronic communications is a rapidly growing part of workstation processing. The tasks performed today are merely a forerunner of what will be done tomorrow. Therefore, self-assessment of this, and other, areas should be a repetitive process, not a one-time occurrence.

A checklist for performing a self-assessment of electronic interfaces is provided in Fig. 9-4. The checklist is constructed so that "yes" responses in-

Item	Response			
	Yes	No	N/A	Comments
1. Does the workstation have communication access to other workstations and/or networks? (If the answer is no, the other questions can be skipped.)				
2. Does the workstation use electronic mail?				
3. Does the workstation use the electronic filing cabinet facility?				
4. Does the workstation use the electronic in-basket?				
5. Does the workstation use the electronic mail memo process?				
6. Are decisions made electronically using workstations?				
7. Does the workstation take advantage of electronic conferences?				
8. Does the workstation utilize electronic billboards?				
9. Does the workstation receive and send data through uploading and downloading?				
10. Is the workstation connected to facilities external to the organization in which the workstation is located?				
11. Does the workstation utilize the electronic telephone book and automatic dialing?				
12. Does the workstation user know how to use the electronic interface facilities?				
13. Has a baseline of interface/communications been established for existing tasks?				
14. Have electronic alternatives been considered for each of the tasks in the baseline?				
15. Are the recipients of communication of the workstation user connected electronically to the workstation?				
16. Are there electronic communication/interface opportunities that the workstation user has not taken advantage of?				

Fig. 9-4. The electronic interface self-assessment checklist.

dicate good electronic interface practices, while "no" responses are areas that should be explored to expand electronic communications.

WORKSTATION RULE OF THUMB

A line from a popular song implies that tomorrow is nice because it's a day away. This is not a good motto for using electronic communication capabilities. The motto should be: "Never put off until tomorrow what you can do today."

Chapter 10

Action 8: Identify
and Use Technicians

One definition of a wise man is one who knows what he does not know. A man who is even wiser uses an expert to compensate for that lack of knowledge.

This chapter explains how to get the right person to help you master the workstation, at the right time. No one needs to fight the workstation war alone. There is help available, and it should be used. This chapter explains the strategies for identifying that help, and then provides the methodology for building a help program for your workstation operation.

Many people believe that computer technology is very difficult to learn. This need not be true. As you use the workstation, you might feel overwhelmed at times, as you try to perform complex or new tasks. Problems that confront even the most experienced workstation users confirm this notion that computers are difficult to use. You might occasionally feel like a motorist on a dark, lonely road, who, after the engine stops running for no apparent reason, kicks the tires in disgust. (Please don't kick the computer—it might break.)

REALISTIC TECHNICAL HELP EXPECTATIONS

A technical expert is defined as someone who understands something about workstation technology that you do not know. However, do not expect this person to help you solve a specific business problem. The technician can explain how the technology works, but not necessarily what it should be used for. Therefore, the responsibility for the proper functioning of the workstation rests with you, not the technician.

You do not understand all of the functions of your own body. When there are problems, you go to a doctor. The doctor provides a diagnosis, offers medicine, and advice. However, the doctor does not have the responsibility for the ultimate health of the patient, just the responsibility to provide good technical advice and a reasonable practice of medicine. The patient must determine that something appears to be wrong, and then seek the advice of the doctor. The doctor rarely knows there is a problem until consulted. After the doctor diagnoses the problem, and offers a solution, the patient takes charge of the situation. The patient does not have to accept or follow the advice, and can seek the advice of another doctor.

The same concept is applicable to the workstation technician. You are free to consult with the technician, and should get sound technical advice, but the ultimate decision on what to do rests with you. Hopefully, the technical advice will be good, but it will not solve your business situation. For example, although the technician might recommend that you acquire a new software package, the urgencies of the business problems do not allow the time to implement the technician's solution.

The following are some realistic expectations of using a technician to:

- Explain procedures and methods. The technician understands how the workstation functions. In some instances, the technician will have to investigate to identify specific steps, but the technician should be able to explain what is necessary to get the workstation to perform the desired functions.
- Explain hardware operation. The mechanical function of pushing buttons, mounting paper, entering disks, etc., are understood by the technician. If you have problems or misunderstandings about the functioning of the hardware, the technician can provide ready answers to these problems.
- Interpret diagnostic. *Diagnostic* messages are information provided by the workstation systems to indicate potential operating problems. The workstation manuals should explain the diagnostic, and what you need to do when that diagnostic message appears. However, if you do not understand the meaning of the diagnostic message, or action to take, then call the technician to help explain this message to you.
- Analyze problems. This is probably one of the greatest roles of the technician. If the unexplained or unexpected happens, the technician should be able to identify why it happened and what to do about it. If problems occur, it is good practice for you to carefully document the problem characteristics. The technician will need this type of information to determine the cause of the problem and recommend a solution.
- Advise on opportunities. There are many ways in which workstations, and the capabilities provided by workstations, can be used on the job. Although the technicians might not know the exact characteristics of your job, they should

be able to advise on how to accomplish your objectives. This advice can relate to the use of the hardware, software or a combination of both, as well as how to fit some of those capabilities into the fulfillment of job tasks. The more experienced technicians can be most helpful in this advice area.

THE USE AND ABUSE OF TECHNICIANS

The proper use of technicians is an art. Overreliance and overuse of the technician can be just as harmful as failing to call upon the technician for help. You should spend some time analyzing and trying to fix your problem before you call a technician. Of course, there are times when you know you really need help.

Learning how to use a workstation effectively involves going through the workstation learning curve. It is similar to learning how to ride a bicycle —it is difficult to do right the first time. On the other hand, until your parents let go of the bicycle, you don't really learn how to do it. Overreliance on the technician can inhibit you in learning to master the workstation skills, because you never have to work out a problem.

A typical problem in dealing with any expert is accepting and following advice about what is needed to do the job right. One of the major challenges in life is a transfer of knowledge from the skilled to the unskilled. Everyone knows that a little knowledge can be dangerous, and, once acquired, the individual might not want to listen to any more advice. It is similar to being given a bottle of medicine by a doctor to cure an illness. You are told to take so much medicine per day until the bottle is empty. The advice sounds good while you feel ill, and you continue taking it until the symptoms seem to disappear. When you begin to feel good, you no longer want to finish the medicine in the bottle. Many medicine bottles remain half-full because the patient starts to feel good. Then when the illness reoccurs, the patient is surprised, even though the doctor's advice was not completely followed. Using consultants frequently involves swallowing more medicine than you really want to take. The general rules for calling for help from a technician are:

- Determine that there is a problem. The technician should not be called until there is a specific problem to be addressed.
- Document the problem characteristics. Whether it is information wanted, or a problem to be solved, the technician should not be called until the specific characteristics of the problem can be identified. It is often better to do this formally, by documenting the symptoms on a piece of paper, rather than relying upon your memory.
- Call the proper technician. Not every technician knows the solution to every problem. Frequently, technicians specialize within the the technical area. For example, some technicians might only know certain software packages. Calling the appropriate technician is the same as calling the appropriate doctor to diagnose or cure a specific physical ailment.

• State the specific objectives to be accomplished by the technician. Frequently the technicians do not know why they have been called. It should be clear from the outset what the technician is being asked to do, and how it will be known when the technician has fulfilled that job. For example, if you are unable to produce the expected output from a software package and you want a technician to help, you should make it clear that when the desired output has been produced, the technician will no longer be needed.

STRATEGIES FOR IDENTIFYING AND USING TECHNICIANS

You have probably experienced moving to a new area to live. When this happens, you are confronted with having to select a new group of technicians to help you. You need doctors, dentists, pharmacists, television repair people, accountants, and other specialists to help you in the event of problems. You will be faced with exactly the same dilemma when you get your workstation. The workstation is an unfamiliar location, and you need a group of technicians to help if you have problems.

The two sources that you can use to locate potential technicians are to obtain them from a knowledgeable source, or to conduct an investigation. For example, in locating a doctor, you might go to a local American Medical Association chapter and ask for a list of doctors, or you might investigate potential doctors by asking friends for recommendation. There are six strategies that you can use to help identify technicians for use in problem solving, listed in Fig. 10-1.

Strategy 1: Information Center. An information center is a resource established by an organization to assist beginners in the use of data processing and related facilities. Not all companies have an information center. It might

Number	Strategy	Description
1.	Information center	A facility established in an organization to help users of data processing facilities who are not data processing professionals.
2.	Vendor technical staff	Members of a vendor's organization whose purpose is to assist the users of the vendor's products.
3.	Help desk/central data processing support	A hot line or individual(s) to contact for help with workstation-related problems.
4.	Prerecorded hot line	A prerecorded telephone message of information of value to the workstation user.
5.	Investigation	Inquiry and study undertaken for the purpose of identifying some needed information.
6.	Recommendation	Reliance upon the advice of another person for sources of reliable technical assistance.

Fig. 10-1. Strategies to identify and use technicians.

or might not be a part of the central data processing facility. At a minimum, it is a function whose primary purpose is to work with people inexperienced in data processing. The amount and extent of help that the information center provides will depend upon its mission and staffing.

The initial purpose for establishing the information center was to assist individuals in the acquisition and use of microcomputers. The workstation is a logical extension of the microcomputer, and thus falls within the information center responsibilities. In many organizations, you must actually go to the information center for assistance, but in a few organizations the information center technical staff will come to your location to help you.

The role and mission of the information center is normally well defined. A simple inquiry can provide information regarding the type and extent of help that you can get from the information center.

Strategy 2: Vendor Technical Staff. Most vendors provide some sort of assistance to users of their products. Therefore, you should identify the vendors of the products in use at the workstation. If problems occur with those products, vendor assistance might be available to help. Some vendors provide hot lines, some will provide on-site assistance if the customer business warrants this assistance, and in some instances organizations contract with vendors for help.

The vendor assistance is not always limited to the vendor's products. Sometimes the assistance will be general to help the customer, in the hope of additional business. For example, the vendor for workstation equipment might assist in office layout. The added service is similar to that of a department store interior decorator who will help a customer with design problems, in the hope that the customer will buy furnishings from the organization.

Strategy 3: Help Desk/Data Processing Support. Most centralized data processing functions include services designed to help the customers of data processing services. One of these services, frequently called the "help desk," is designed to provide assistance to users having problems with technical data processing. Many centralized data processing functions are establishing workstation support facilities.

The type of support provided by the central group might be similar to an outside vendor. For example, the workstation support staff might establish a "hot line" which you can call for help, or they might be available for you to visit, sit down, and talk about your problems.

Strategy 4: Prerecorded Hot Line. Some organizations provide information about central processing of interest to users. For example, you might have established access to centralized databases. If the databases are not operational, workstation processing will be affected. Prerecorded hot line messages provide quick information to you about the problem, and might tell when the facility will be back in operation. You call a hot line telephone number when you experience a problem affecting the central site, to get information about the resolution of that problem. It might be impractical for the central site to notify all users directly when they are experiencing problems, and thus they install a hot line facility for that purpose.

Strategy 5: Investigation. Investigation is all of the inquiry activities that you undertake to identify good technical assistance. Investigation can involve talking to other workstation users, going to data processing seminars and conferences, researching local support facilities, and questioning technicians about assistance, and for sources of other technical assistance.

Strategy 6: Recommendation. One of the favorite methods to identify technical assistance is obtaining the recommendations of respected colleagues. Workstation users might be provided a list of potential technical assistants, or such a list might be obtained from other workstation users, or a users group. Just as you select many of your personal technicians, such as family doctors, by recommendation, you should solicit advice about technical assistants for your workstation problems.

ACQUIRING AND USING TECHNICAL HELP

The point at which you need a technician is not the time to look for one, just as you should not begin to look for a doctor after you get sick. The technician, like the doctor, should be known, so that when the problem occurs, it is only a matter of calling the technician for help.

The methodology proposed in this chapter is one of identifying a list of technical help by category of problem. The use of the technician will occur when the problem occurs, from a list of names and phone numbers. A four-step method for identifying technicians to use when problems occur is outlined in Fig. 10-20.

Step 1: Identify Potential Areas Requiring Technical Assistance. This step requires the division of problems into categories. A suggested framework of problems has been provided in Fig. 10-3. This list is designed to be completed before problems occur.

The problem areas have been divided into hardware problems, existing application problems, communication system problems (e.g., telephone lines), systems design advice, new application advice, and all other (specific problem areas should be identified individually).

Step 2: Identify Sources of Technical Assistance. The strategies for locating technical assistance described earlier in this chapter should be used to identify potential technical help. This list should grow over time. Use this list to select your technical advisors.

If there are problem areas with no technicians identified, additional investigation might need to be undertaken. At least one technician for each problem area should be identified, although the same individual might be able to provide technical assistance in more than one problem area.

Step 3: Investigate and Select the Desired Technician. If more than one technician is available to assist with a problem area, the most desir-

Number	Step	Description	Responsibilities
1.	Identify list of potential areas requiring technical assistance.	The general categories of problems should be identified so that technicians can be associated with those areas of concern.	○ Workstation developers ○ Workstation user
2.	Identify sources of technical assistance.	The technicians that can be called upon for assistance should be identified (information center, vendor technical staff, help desk/central data processing support, prerecorded hot line, investigation, recommendation).	○ Workstation user
3.	Investigate and select desired technicians.	The workstation user must determine which technicians are most qualified to help in the event of a problem.	○ Workstation user
4.	Prepare Technician Call-In List.	A list should be prepared indicating which technician will be called for specific problem areas.	○ Workstation user

Fig. 10-2. Methods for identifying and using technicians.

able should be selected and recorded on the Technician Call-In List (Fig. 10-3) In some instances, it might be desirable to list several technicians in the order in which they would be called. This can be helpful if the desired technician is not available at the time needed. The selection will be by individual preference, but should include the following criteria:

- Availability to help.
- Technical expertise.
- Compatability with user.

Step 4: Prepare Technician Call-In List. Based upon the selection criteria, the Technician Call-In List should be completed. The name of the technician(s) to be called in the event of a particular problem should be recorded on the call-in list. The list should also indicate how that technician can be located.

The Technician Call-In List should be kept within easy reach. When a problem occurs, you must first identify the problem area. You can then refer to the Technician Call-In List, locate the appropriate technician, and call for the needed assistance to help you solve your problem.

USING TECHNICAL HELP:
IMPEDIMENTS AND COUNTERSTRATEGIES

There are three primary impediments to the use of technicians. The first is cost. If the services of the technician cost money, the expenditure might appear to outweigh the benefits derived from the technical advice. In some instances, vendor technicians are only available under an annual service contract, making it necessary to calculate value before problems have occurred.

The counterstrategy is to weigh costs against benefits. The benefit of the

Number	Problem Area	Technician	How To Locate
1.	Hardware		
2.	Applications (existing)		
	a)		
	b)		
	c)		
	d)		
	e)		
	f)		
	g)		
	h)		
3.	Communication		
4.	Systems design advice (customization)		
5.	New application advice		
6.	Other		

Fig. 10-3. A form to create the technician call-in list.

service to be provided should be estimated. It is only after benefits have been estimated that you can decide whether it is worth the cost to engage a technician.

The second impediment is the "I'd rather do it myself" attitude. Some people just like to work out their own problems. They don't feel comfortable with technicians, and only want to call them in a dire emergency. This impediment can result in not calling a technician when a technician should be called.

The counterstrategy is to predetermine call-in situations. You should predetermine when it is advisable to call a technician. When these instances occur, the technicians should be called. This provides a logical basis for making decisions, avoiding situation-by-situation determinations about whether you should call in a technician.

The final impediment involves a lack of technician credibility. The reputation of technicians might be tarnished by opinions and stories about the capability of that individual. When it is time to call a technician, you might be reluctant to call that person because of problems other people have encountered in similar situations.

The counterstrategy is to select technicians before the problems occur. Specific problem-solving objectives should be established before engaging a technician. These objectives should be defined in-depth with a technician, and an informal contract agreed upon. In these instances, technicians who do not feel qualified might disqualify themselves from service, but at a minimum there is a basis for evaluation of technical services.

SELF-ASSESSMENT CHECKLIST

The effective use of technicians can be a great aid in mastering workstation technology. Most users experience some difficult problems during their use of the workstation. Being able to call upon assistance can be a great comfort when working with a new and complex technology.

A self-assessment checklist to help you measure the effectiveness of your planned ability to use technicians is provided in Fig. 10-4. This checklist is designed so that "yes" responses indicate practices designed to use technical assistance effectively. The "no" responses should cause you to reconsider how you use technical assistance in the performance of your workstation tasks.

WORKSTATION RULE OF THUMB

It is generally not an effective use of your time to solve technical problems. Managers should use technicians to solve technical problems, leaving managers free to address managerial problems.

Item	Response			
	Yes	No	N/A	Comments
1. Have the areas of potential workstation problems been identified?				
2. Has the need for technical help in each of those areas been assessed?				
3. Has the use of an information center for technical assistance been evaluated?				
4. Has the use of vendor technical staff or assistance been evaluated?				
5. Has a help desk or central data processing support personnel been evaluated for potential technical assistance?				
6. Has a prerecorded hot line been evaluated for potential technical assistance?				
7. Have you conducted adequate investigation to identify individuals and resources for technical assistance?				
8. Have respected colleagues been interviewed to identify potential technical assistance?				
9. Has at least one source of technical assistance been identified for each potential problem area?				
10. Have you conducted sufficient investigation to determine which of the potential technical resources would be most suited to your needs?				
11. Has a Technician Call-In List been prepared?				
12. Is the list close to the workstation in the event that it is needed?				
13. Are alternative technical sources included on the call-in list in the event that the desired technician is unavailable?				

Fig. 10-4. The technical help self-assessment checklist.

Chapter 11

Action 9: Make Quality Your Number-One Priority

Quality means doing it right the first time. The cost of not doing it right the first time might be the abandonment of the workstation.

This chapter emphasizes the need for quality in the workstation program. A quest for quality does not preclude experimentation and elimination of the learning curve. However, it must be the cornerstone of the workstation system, for that system to achieve the optimum payback. Some of these quality concepts have been discussed in earlier chapters.

Quality might be the most important product that an organization possesses. Many people believe that a large number of today's corporations will not be in business in a few years if they fail to give quality the highest priority in their corporation. The worldwide competition now going on will quickly put the non-quality competitors out of business. The lesson learned by the American automotive industry, which lost sales to non-U.S. companies due to poor quality, will occur in other companies whose products fail to meet the quality and price of its competitors.

Quality should not be viewed in the context of relative goodness or high cost. Quality means meeting requirements or expectations. Quality products must be produced that cost less than competitors, but perform better. This will require some new methods of doing work. Workstations will be one of these methods.

WHY QUALITY WORK IS DIFFICULT TO ACHIEVE

Everybody is in favor of quality. It would be difficult to find anyone who did not want, or support, or attempt to achieve quality work. People do not set out deliberately to do poor-quality work. Why, then, don't people achieve quality, if it is so desirable a goal?

The answer to that is quite simple. People have different definitions of quality. Quality to one person is frequently junk to another. The problem occurs because the people involved in the quality decision do not agree on what quality means. Unless it is well-defined and measurable, it will be an argumentative attribute. There are three major reasons why there are quality problems.

Problem 1: Product Did Not Meet User Expectation. In this case, the user expected something different than the developer planned to produce. For example, a consumer might expect that all problems with a product will be corrected, even though it is never implied or specified, and when the developer refuses to fix a specific problem, it is upsetting to the consumer.

In other cases, it is a misunderstanding. The developer never planned to build the product the way the user expected it to be built. There was absolutely no probability that the user would think that a quality product was produced.

Problem 2: Luck of the Draw on Defects. Some products are built to include a certain level of defects. For example, part A might be acceptable if only one out of 1,000 fail, and part B might be acceptable if only one out of 2,000 fail, and part C, if one out of 500 fail. The quality tolerances could be met, and yet a user could obtain a product that had a defective part A, B, and C in the same product. While this is highly unlikely, it occurs. People getting this product often refer to it as a "lemon."

Problem 3: Failure to Define Quality. The major problem in quality is that it might not be defined. It is the undefined requirement that causes most of the problems. Often, the user never defines the desired level of quality. The product that is developed is what is delivered.

The underlying theme in quality problems is the lack of a realistic and well-defined level of quality. Most quality problems can be overcome by a rigorous definition of quality. Once that definition has been documented and agreed to, quality problems tend to disappear.

```
WORKSTATION RULE OF THUMB

The lack of quality is a management problem, not
a technical problem. Without strong management
support, quality does not happen.
```

WHAT MAKES QUALITY WORK?

To make quality work, it must be a way of life rather than a set of quality standards. Both management and workers must be dedicated to quality. It must truly be the cornerstone of the organization. The emphasis on quality should come from senior management. It is often the chief executive officer of the organization who must provide the direction. This direction should be expressed as a quality policy of the organization.

The principles that make quality work are rarely taught in managerial programs. Invariably, the emphasis in managerial strategies is on productivity and profit-making, not quality. It is difficult to change that way of thinking to one which emphasizes quality first, and is willing to let productivity and profit be subordinate to the quality emphasis. It is particularly hard when boards of directors and stockholders are putting emphasis on quarterly profits.

The following are the three keys to a quality environment:

- Managerial emphasis on quality. This is the most important, because without strong management support, quality just does not happen. There can be pockets of quality in an organization, but without the support of senior management, other priorities take precedence over quality.
- Well-defined processes. Quality is difficult to control unless there is a well-defined process for producing products. It matters little whether the product is a letter, an automobile, or a computer program. If the product is not made by a predefined process, variables cannot be changed, and the effect of change cannot be measured. Without a continual improvement of the processes, quality will rarely improve.
- Quantitative measurement of quality. Quality is either there, or it is not there; there are no degrees of quality. For example, a baker selling donuts by the dozen would go out of business if his staff continually packed donuts in groups of 15 or 10. Fifteen is not a better quality dozen donuts than are 10 donuts. Quality is meeting standards, and in a dozen donuts, the standard is 12. Any quantity other than twelve is a defect.

Eventually, quality must be measured. The practice of measurement is known as *statistical quality control.* It requires that measurable objectives be established, and then have someone determine whether or not those objectives have been achieved. If they are not achieved, the variances from the objective or standard should be investigated, and the processes changed to help eliminate that defect when the product is again produced.

What Does Quality Theory Have to Do With Me?

There are two cornerstones in the policy of organizations that have made quality their central theme. The first is the emphasis on quality by the organization, and the second is that quality is everybody's responsibility. If you do not require quality of your own work, it will not happen. Thus, it is important that, first, you emphasize quality in your workstation processing, and, second, that you accept the quality of workstation processing as your responsibility.

This acceptance of quality will cause you to be more concerned about the quality of work you do than the speed in which you perform the tasks, particularly in the beginning—speed will come after quality has been achieved. You will become a "complainer" when your support equipment and software fails to meet quality expectations. You will not be satisfied with equipment that breaks down, or software that fails to perform correctly. You will be an advocate for improvement of quality in these support services. You will demand quality from your subordinates and colleagues who interact with you in the workstation network. For example, colleagues or subordinates who fail to respond to electronic messages will become unacceptable, and ineffective use of the capabilities by your colleagues and workers will become unacceptable. You will demand reliability in the data that you receive and transmit in the communication network.

STRATEGIES TO IMPLEMENT WORKSTATION QUALITY

Strategies for ensuring quality should be based on senior management policies. The implementation of those quality strategies at all levels of the organization makes workstation quality happen. You do not look at workstations, and decide that among all organizational activities, this is where quality should occur. Quality should be predominant throughout the organization, so that workstation processing is just another activity subject to the same quality standards as any other activity.

The quality strategies must be viewed differently than many of the other strategies described in this book. In some of the chapters, a shopping basket of strategies was provided, with the option for you to pick and choose among the strategies. However, for the quality strategies, the whole package should be implemented. Quality is a very complex topic, requiring a multidisciplined approach to make it work. There are six strategies that are needed to make quality happen in an organization, listed in Fig. 11-1.

Strategy 1: Avoid Numerical Goals. A person can only have one mas-

Number	Strategy	Description
1.	Avoid numerical goals.	Emphasis should be on achieving quality, not accomplishing numerical objectives.
2.	Provide workstation training.	Untrained users cannot be expected to produce quality work.
3.	Provide quality statistical control training.	Each user should understand basic statistical quality control measurement.
4.	Use quality vendors exclusively.	Dealing with quality vendors will ensure that the vendor workstation products will not cause lower quality standards.
5.	Reduce fear.	Fear is one of the greatest inhibitors of quality. It forces individuals to switch emphasis to justifying and protecting their jobs, as opposed to producing quality products.
6.	Reduce interdepartmental conflict.	There should be consistency of purpose among departments so that they are working toward the same goals, and are not competitive.

Fig. 11-1. Strategies for quality workstation processing.

125

ter. If achieving numerical goals is that master, then quality cannot be number one to that person. Management must choose between quality and numerical goals.

Some organizations run on numerical goals. Their expectation is that workers will produce a predetermined number of products, achieve them at a predetermined date, or produce a product in a certain number of minutes or hours. Turning this philosophy of numerical objectives to one of quality objectives is a significant change in managerial thinking.

This policy is not inconsistent with establishing quantitative quality standards. The emphasis is to use numbers to measure quality, as opposed to producing "things." The key to this strategy is that when the process is properly adjusted to control quality, the number of products per unit of work will increase.

Strategy 2: Workstation Training. Real estate agents state that the three primary attributes of a piece of real estate are "location, location, and location." In ensuring the quality of an individual's work, the three key ingredients should be "training, training, and more training." It only makes sense that fully trained people perform better on the job than untrained people.

Training should include both teaching of skills and evaluation of mastery of those skills. It is not enough to teach. Management must be sure that individuals have mastered the skills. This will require a demonstration by you that you have mastered workstation skills.

After someone has been trained and demonstrated mastery of skills, only minimal supervision is needed. The primary purpose of supervision should be to perform supervisory tasks, not ensuring that individuals perform their work properly. If the individuals have been trained and evaluated, management should be freed from worrying about performance, to devoting their efforts to planning even higher levels of quality.

Being a manager and using new sophisticated technology, you probably will not be trained, supervised, or evaluated by your management in workstation skills. However, the quality principle still applies. You need training, and then you need some qualified person to confirm that you have adequately mastered the skills. With this new technology, you might be making mistakes in performance and not know it. Only evaluation and additional training will correct these operational deficiencies.

Strategy 3: Quality Statistical Control Training. There are two aspects of quality. The first deals with ensuring that the processes provided offer the highest probability of success. The second aspect is ensuring that the products of that process are quality products. This latter activity is called *quality control.*

Statistical quality control uses simple but powerful statistical principles to help determine if quality has been achieved. The basis of statistical quality control is to first establish quality standards, and then measure performance against those standards. Deviations from acceptable levels of work are then

126

analyzed statistically. The objective is to determine whether the variances are due to chance, or whether they identify a pattern of defective performance.

This sounds complex, but it need not be. For example, careful record keeping and analysis might show that you are experiencing delays in transmission between three and four every afternoon. Because this occurs every day, you could assume that there is some condition that causes this to happen. You can then develop a counterstrategy, such as performing your communication at an earlier or later time each day.

The evaluation of performance will determine the type of action that needs to be taken. If no problems occur, no action needs to be taken. If the defects are random, the solution is normally more training. For example, you might not have understood the procedures or exercised the proper precautions during operations. On the other hand, if the defects reveal patterns, it is more likely that the process itself is either causing or contributing to the defect. In that instance, the process needs to be changed.

Statistical methods should help you perform your own quality control practices. It is important to understand the basic statistical measures such as mean, median, mode, and standard deviation in order to properly evaluate groups of problems. Many times, by just recording the problem data, the solution becomes obvious, if you possess a few basic statistical skills. When the cause of the problem is determined, you can involve all of the people needed to fix the problem. A team effort might be needed to fix a process problem.

Strategy 4: Use Quality Vendors Exclusively. Vendors make an important contribution to the quality of workstation processing. In some installations, almost the entire workstation capability is provided by the vendor. Vendor products include workstation hardware, software, and communication facilities. In addition, vendors might provide training, consulting, and system customization.

There are many options that an organization has in selecting and working with vendors. The recommended method is to work only with vendors who can demonstrate the quality of their work. Vendors who cannot demonstrate how they ensure the quality of their products should be excluded from all negotiations.

Experience has shown that it sometimes costs two to three times the price of the product to install it. This cost can increase significantly if the product is defective. A higher price on the vendor product might be paid back many times by not having to deal with product problems.

The principles in this book regarding workstation quality should be applied to vendor relations. At a minimum, a vendor should be able to demonstrate that:

- A quality control function has been established within the vendor's organization.
- Quality standards for the product being acquired have been defined.
- Test results show that the product being acquired has achieved the desired quality standards.

If the quality of the product is critical to the success of the workstation program, it might be desirable to visit the vendor's site. This on-site visit will permit an evaluation of the vendor's activities. If there are doubts about the quality, this extra effort might produce substantial benefits. Normally, these visits will be done by technicians, unless it is the business functions of a product where quality is important. In that case, you might want to personally visit the vendor site.

Strategy 5: Reduce Fear. People have difficulty functioning effectively when they live in fear. Fear can be caused by the threat of losing a job, losing prestige, or losing opportunity. It might also mean ridicule by one's peers.

Fear is one of the greatest deterrents to quality work. In a quality environment, employees must be open about process flaws and defects. If people are concerned about their jobs or credibility, it is difficult to be open about the types of problems they are having on the job. If fear is removed from the environment, the individual is free to do whatever is necessary to improve the quality of work. There is also no concern about the loss of jobs associated with significant increases in productivity. You should lobby for open and fear-free discussions in your company on workstation processes and practices.

Strategy 6: Reduce Departmental Conflict. Departments that are in conflict rarely work effectively toward the accomplishment of common goals. Conflict tends to lead to finger-pointing. Departments become more concerned with their own growth and reputation than with the quality of the products of the organization.

The establishment of workstation processing is normally the work of many departments. For example, data processing might establish the basic hardware configurations and software tools, the office services department might provide the physical facilities, the communications department might provide the communication interfaces and software, and a special workstation support team might provide the technical advice and counseling. The user must provide some of the requirements and, of course, the day-to-day operation.

All of these people need to be working together to produce quality processing. At a minimum, this means some commonly agreed-to objectives, and an agreement of purpose among all related departments for achieving those objectives. It generally requires both a coordinating group to oversee the program, and managerial support to encourage cooperation, not conflict.

WORKSTATION RULE OF THUMB
Quality in workstation processing is a team effort, not an individual effort.

ENSURING QUALITY

A five-step process to assist you in ensuring the quality of your workstation processing is shown in Fig. 10-2.

Number	Step	Description	Responsibilities
1.	Establish your personal quality policy.	Document your intent regarding quality of workstation processing (avoid numerical goals, reduce fear, reduce departmental conflict).	○ Workstation users
2.	Set quality objectives (standards for the workstation).	Identify measurable quality objectives for workstation processing (workstation training, reduce fear).	○ Workstation users ○ User management
3.	Establish processes to accomplish quality standards.	Develop a process to produce the desired measurable quality objects (quality statistical control training, reduce departmental conflict).	○ Workstation systems group
4.	Establish quality control procedures to ensure quality is achieved.	Install a quality control program to oversee and ensure the quality objectives are achieved (quality statistical control training, use quality vendors exclusively, reduce departmental conflict).	○ Workstation users ○ Workstation systems group
5.	Investigate and determine the cause for all defects (i.e., variances from quality standards).	No defect is too small to investigate. It is only through defect identification and correction that quality can be improved (workstation training, quality statistical control training, reduce departmental conflict).	○ Workstation users ○ Workstation systems group

Fig. 11-2. Ensuring the quality of workstation processing.

Step 1: Establish Your Personal Quality Policy. A quality policy defines your intent regarding quality. If you want quality, you should make a positive statement to that effect. For workstation processing, the quality policy might be a redefinition of a higher level quality policy.

The following four items would make an ideal quality policy for you:

- Provide products and services which are free of defects.
- Learn to do things right the first time.
- Make sure that each job, each stage of the process, is free of defects.
- Remember that quality is my job and responsibility.

Step 2: Set Quality Objectives. The only method to close the expectation gap and ensure a standard level of quality between the various groups is to use a stringent definition of quality. Until measurable *quality objectives* (i.e., quality standards) are established, quality remains an elusive concept. Once defined, expectations are all centered around known quality objectives. Don't accept workstation junk. Ask what the quality standards are for the products you receive.

The most important purpose for establishing measurable objectives is to ensure that you achieve what you expect to achieve. This can be accomplished by using a process that establishes quality objectives for the work you undertake, then monitoring the process to make sure that you are achieving the desired quality. Without measurable objectives, the assessment of quality becomes judgmental. This requires expert judges, who are normally not available.

Step 3: Establish Processes to Accomplish Quality Standards. The development of processes is the responsibility of both the group developing the workstation and you. The workstation development group has the primary responsibility for defining the processes. However, you might need to customize that process based upon your specific quality and business objectives. Chapters 5, 7, and 9 in this book have defined the types of processes that are needed for workstations.

Step 4: Establish Quality Control Procedures to Ensure that Quality Is Achieved. Quality control is your responsibility. However, the development of the quality control can be done by the team that develops the workstation processes. Included with each process should be a method for evaluating the quality of its product.

There are many types of quality control tools that you could use, including:

- Self-assessment checklists.
- Checkpoints at which the status of your work can be determined, for example, a check against a control total.
- Diagnostics indicating the status of work (both correct and incorrect).
- Standards or yardsticks against which results can be measured (e.g., ratios or expected relationships between two or more variables).

130

• Lists of types and quantities of products or information to be produced (e.g., reports, documents, or processing results).

Step 5: Investigate and Determine the Cause of All Defects. A quality objective is to produce defect-free products and services. This aspect of quality cannot be achieved if defects become the accepted norm. It is only through the investigation of all defects that the processes can be continually improved. You must either accept defects as a normal part of processing, or not accept them, in which case they must be investigated, and appropriate action taken. Even if the action is to do nothing, the defect should be recorded, so that the cumulative effect of multiple occurrences of the same type of defect will be known.

WORKSTATION QUALITY: IMPEDIMENTS AND COUNTERSTRATEGIES

The major impediment to quality is that it is not the first priority in the minds of individuals responsible for the work. When other items take a higher priority, quality suffers.

One major impediment to quality is the reliance on budgets. Budgets allocate the resources available to produce a product. If an individual is charged with meeting the budget, then that individual must evaluate the consequences of not meeting the budget. If the consequences of not meeting the budget are more severe than not meeting quality, the individual will meet the budget and quality will suffer.

The counterstrategy is to plan for quality objectives in the budget. Clearly establishing quality objectives makes it difficult to "cheat" on those objectives in order to meet a budget limit. Budgets are only meaningful when people are also held accountable for the level of quality required with the approved funding.

Equally deadly to meeting quality objectives are schedules. A scheduled completion date poses the same threat to quality that budgets do. The individual held accountable for meeting a schedule suffers from the same quality dilemma imposed by meeting budget limitations. When the two impediments are coupled, quality normally ends up the loser.

The counterstrategy is to stress schedules in quality policy. Management's quality policies must put quality in the proper perspective. Without a very apparent alternative to schedules and budgets, quality will not be number one.

SELF-ASSESSMENT CHECKLIST

The self-assessment of workstation quality is a quality control practice. A checklist is a quality control tool. It is another step in assuring the quality of workstation processing.

A workstation quality control checklist is provided in Fig. 11-3. The checklist is designed so that "yes" responses indicate good quality practices. The

Item	Response			
	Yes	No	N/A	Comments
1. Has senior management established a quality policy for the organization?				
2. Has that quality policy been interpreted for workstation processing?				
3. Do the quality strategies avoid reliance on numerical goals?				
4. Are workstation users trained in the needed workstation skills?				
5. Are workstation users evaluated to ensure that they have mastered workstation skills?				
6. Are managers trained in basic statistical quality control methods?				
7. Are vendors required to demonstrate their quality control methods?				
8. Are vendor negotations limited to those vendors who can demonstrate that they have adequate quality control methods?				
9. Does management strategy attempt to reduce employee fear?				
10. Does management strategy attempt to reduce the interdepartmental conflict?				
11. Is someone responsible for the quality of workstation processing?				
12. Have measurable quality objectives been established for workstation processing?				
13. Are processes developed for performing the tasks assigned to workstations?				
14. Are the processes capable of achieving the quality objectives?				
15. Are the quality objectives stated in measurable terms?				
16. Are there quality control procedures in place to monitor the level of quality produced?				
17. Are all defects investigated to determine whether changes need to be made to the process and/or product to achieve the desired level of quality?				

Fig. 11-3. The workstation quality self-assessment checklist.

"no" responses should be investigated to determine whether improvements can be made to the process and/or the product.

WORKSTATION RULE OF THUMB

Quality not only means doing it right the first time, but also doing the right task from a business perspective.

Chapter 12

Action 10: Use the New Methods

There is little value in providing a manager with a tool which will not be used—or used effectively!

This chapter emphasizes the importance of using the new methods. Your proficiency in using workstation technology will only occur with practice.

Change is one of the greatest impediments to progress. People hate change. Even those organizations that make a living by introducing change hate to have change imposed on the way they work. The old expression "you can lead a horse to water but you can't make him drink" is very appropriate to the introduction of new technology. Change appears doubly difficult when new methods are coupled with new technology.

CHANGING THE WAY MANAGERS DO WORK

The introduction of the managerial workstation will have a significant impact on the way managers perform their work. The manager has been immune from computer processing during the first part of the computer age. The workstation now thrusts the manager into the forefront of computer technology.

The workstation might be the single greatest productivity tool for performance of the managerial function. For the first time, the manager personally will have access to the power of the computer. Up until this point, the emphasis has been on using the computer to improve the productivity of the manager's staff, clerical functions, and the factory, but not the manager.

The real key to office productivity is making the manager manage. Freeing the manager from time-consuming clerical tasks will provide more time for organizing, planning, and controlling. One company changed the title from manager to leader, because they wanted people who would lead their subordinates.

The workstation will also affect the way managers interact and conduct business. Currently, the manager's time is expended on meetings, telephone calls, and interaction with subordinates. For some managers, the entire workday can be consumed with these activities. Using a workstation, more of this interaction will occur over communication lines and computer processing, rather than in face-to-face discussions.

The key to the entire productivity chain is getting the manager to use the new methods. The motivation to do this must be internal. However, the manager needs a supporting environment to foster that internal motivation.

WORKSTATION RULE OF THUMB

Action, once begun, must be sustained in order to accomplish the stated objective. Many projects are started, but few are finished. Therefore, success is not just starting, but sustaining, an action until the desired results are achieved.

STRATEGIES FOR USING THE NEW METHODS

The strategies for encouraging workstation usage should be supportive strategies, designed to both encourage workstation usage and support the continual effort needed to master the workstation skills. Any new process has discouraging periods associated with it. It is important that the survival strategies provide the right type of support as it is needed. Five recommended support strategies are listed in Fig. 12-1.

Strategy 1: Reward Systems. One key element that is frequently overlooked in any activity is the rewards provided for performing that activity. Too frequently, rewards are viewed only as pay increases, benefit plans, and pensions. Experience has shown, however, that the monetary rewards are really not motivators. The lack of them can cause a lack of motivation, but the presence rarely has any sustained effect on motivation.

A change in the way an individual performs work requires a change in behavior. This is the concept referred to by educators when they want someone to use new concepts and perform new tasks. Unfortunately, behavior change is difficult for most individuals. The most common method for inducing behavior change is punishment. People are told what will happen if they don't do something. For example, a manager might be excluded from the decision-making process if he doesn't use a workstation. This is a form of punishment.

Number	Strategy	Description
1.	Reward systems	Reward the desired behavior, and reprimand, or at least do not reward, undesirable behavior.
2.	Technical support system (e.g., information center)	Provide managers with answers to technical questions and problems when needed.
3.	Consistency of purpose (in processing plan)	Ensure that the use of the workstation is consistent to business objectives and part of an overall managerial plan.
4.	User groups	Form groups of workstation users so that they can be mutually supportive and share information.
5.	Hot line	Provide a source of immediate answers to high-priority problems.

Fig. 12-1. Strategies for using the new methods.

Unfortunately, it's not the best method to encourage behavior change.

Rewards are more effective than punishment in changing behavior. Everyone knows, in training an animal, that rewards for doing desired behavior will get the animal to perform a trick faster than giving punishment for not doing the trick. The same is true with managers, even chief executive officers.

The types of rewards that can be used to encourage the initial and continued use of workstations include the following that you can provide for your staff, and hopefully your manager will provide for you (hint: give your boss a copy of this book):

• Managerial performance appraisal system partially based upon the ability to use the workstation effectively. The manager can be evaluated on the type of tasks, and the quality of those tasks performed on workstations.

• Workstation tasks included in the job description.

• Self-evaluation criteria provided to the manager for personal evaluation. There is a significant reward associated with knowing that you have performed a job well. In order to do this, measurement criteria must be defined, and tools given, to measure performance against that criteria.

• Praise of senior management. A manager's boss, or perhaps someone even higher up should make it known that work performed on a workstation is very much appreciated by senior management. It is extremely helpful to have senior management declare that certain types of behavior are desired and appreciated.

• Increased responsibility. Performing beginning tasks satisfactorily should qualify the manager to perform more sophisticated tasks.

A reward structure tied to performance encourages sustained action. A reward system should be built upon plateaus of performance, so that the more proficient a manager becomes, the greater the personal opportunities provided to that manager.

Strategy 2: Technical Support System. The mastery of workstation technology poses varying degrees of difficulty to different individuals. Some managers will have minimal problems in using workstations, while others will be stretching their capabilities. The support system must address both of these extremes.

The technical support system should be a multilayered system of support. The levels of support that are most effective include the following items, which summarize many of the concepts presented in this book:

• Help screens provided in workstation processing for the user, and activated by entry of a special command by the workstation user. Frequently, this involves typing the word "HELP" on the workstation keyboard. The diagnostics usually explain the procedure that needs to be followed to accomplish a specific task.

• Trouble tips for a workstation user to follow if unsolvable problems occur. For example, if an error message should appear, a trouble tip should indicate what to do to overcome the problem. These troubleshooting diagnostics should address the most common problems that a workstation user might encounter during normal processing. The more extensive these diagnostics, the greater the confidence of the individual in using workstations.

• Procedures manual to provide a detailed, step-by-step procedure on how to perform each task. If the user is uncertain about how to accomplish a certain task, this manual is a ready reference for learning or reinforcing skills.

• Technical advisors to call in the event of problems (as described in Chapter 10). The more specific this list can be, the easier it is for the workstation user to find the right person to call.

• On-site assistance by a technical expert, to be used only when all other measures fail. Knowing that, if all else fails, someone will come and help solve the problem is a very comforting situation.

Strategy 3: Consistency of Purpose. There is a constant stream of messages from management. Some messages say: get the project done within budget, others emphasize quality, and still others are time oriented. One department gets one message, and another department, another. The more fragmented these messages, the more difficult they are to interpret.

Quality is tied to consistency of purpose. When there are diverse directions being given, it is difficult to produce quality products. In this confusing atmosphere, individuals and organizations tend to work against one another because management's objectives are unclear. Consistency of purpose means that the objectives of the organization are well established, and each organizational entity is working toward those objectives. In workstation processing, this means that the workstation is incorporated into a plan that is supportive of the organization's objectives. The manager operating the workstation should clearly understand how workstation processing fits into personal objectives, departmental objectives, and the organization's objectives.

The accomplishment of the consistency of purpose objective is normally achieved through centralized planning. This ensures that the plans of all the individual organizational entities are consistent with the overall organizational plan. The individual manager must also integrate workstation processing into personal planning.

Strategy 4: User Groups. User groups have a long tradition in the data processing area. The purpose of user groups has been to encourage the sharing of information among users. Users enjoy and benefit from talking with other users about common problems.

User groups can be both formal and informal. Informal user groups are casual meetings of users arranged for the purpose of periodically exchanging information. The informal user group meetings can be arranged by individual users or other groups responsible for workstation systems. Formal user groups are normally approved by management.

The types of activities undertaken by user groups, both formal and informal, are:

- Sharing experiences of why things work or don't work.
- Offering solutions to common problems.
- Lobbying for improvement against the organization developing workstation systems, to encourage that organization to take specific action.
- Mutual support to solve specific problems or learn specific capabilities.
- User training sessions to teach other users how to perform specific activities.
- User-developed solutions developed to help other users address certain problems or solve common processing needs.

Strategy 5: Hot Line. Individuals working alone can easily become frustrated. Problems which appear insurmountable to an individual might be normal and routine problems of workstation processing. However, the lack of a solution to those problems might cause someone to abandon workstations.

The hot line is a telephone link to solutions. It provides someone who understands the system, the type of problems that occur, and can relate those problems to user-described symptoms. It becomes the user's lifeline to assistance.

The hot line concept has proved to be extremely beneficial in centralized data processing. Users who could not find the right individual, or had difficulty raising the right question, were provided the needed support through the hot line. This facility, normally located in computer operations, was staffed by senior individuals trained to assist users with problems. It has been credited with improving the credibility of computer operations.

The hot line is usually a single telephone number staffed by an individual who will either give or get the needed answer within a relatively short period of time. Many hot lines establish a two-hour maximum answer to user problems. The hot line operator, normally a senior computer operator, is charged with the responsibility of finding the appropriate individual to answer whatever question is raised. This relatively low-cost facility is frequently what makes the workstation concept work.

ENSURING THAT THE NEW METHODS ARE USED

The effective use of workstations should not be left to chance. The group overseeing the installation of workstations should establish processes to ensure that those workstations are effectively used. If individual managers do not use the workstations, then the group responsible for workstations has failed as much as the individual user.

Managers use workstations when they perceive such use to be of personal value, and do not use them when they believe it is not in their best interest. The process of encouraging the use of workstations must involve motivating individual managers to want to use workstations. However, the use of workstations cannot be forced; it must be encouraged. This poses a special challenge to the group developing workstation procedures. In most organizations, they lack the authority to make people abide by their will, but still have the responsibility of ensuring that workstations are used effectively.

The procedures for ensuring that the new workstation methods are used are listed in Fig. 12-2 together with the strategies that are helpful in accomplishing each step, and the individual responsible for that step.

Step 1: Develop and Publicize a Long-Range Data Processing Plan. Workstations are one part of a sophisticated data processing network. The workstations need to be fed information, and to be able to communicate with other workstations and central processing sites. These networks involve transfer of information, prioritizing work, establishing interface protocols, controlling network access, and providing management over the use of network.

The establishment and operation of a large communication network is a complex operation. Not only is interface and capacity a consideration, but the logical progression from one generation of technology to another must be carefully planned. Without planning, the resulting systems may be underutilized and undermanaged, resulting in the ineffective and uneconomical use of the data processing resources. Planning should occur at the highest level in the organization. Normally, data processing management will take the lead for long-range data processing planning. However, it is advisable that all major departments provide input to the plan. In many organizations, the planning encompasses a five-year period.

Step 2: Establish an Organizational Structure to Support That Plan. Most organizational structures are hierarchical in design. At the same time, data processing networks are flat, and flow between the various branches of the hierarchy. This might mean that the only common office to which all

	Step	Description	Responsibilities
1.	Develop and publicize long-range data processing plan.	Having a plan and making individuals aware of how their tasks fit into that plan increases the importance and meaning of the job, and thus increases motivation and productivity (consistency of purpose).	○ Senior data processing management
2.	Establish an organizational structure to support that plan.	Put into place the support groups necessary to accomplish the long-range data processing plan (technical support system, user groups, hot line).	○ Senior management
3.	Monitor progress against that plan.	Install the necessary quality control procedures to verify whether or not the plan is being accomplished (reward systems, technical support system).	○ Workstation development group
4.	Reward individuals who accomplish the plan's objectives.	Reward the individuals who are accomplishing the plan's objectives, and do not reward those who are not accomplishing the objectives (reward systems).	○ Senior management

Fig. 12-2. Ensuring that the new methods are used.

users of the workstation network report is the president or chief executive officer. Data processing networks run counter to the typical organizational structure, making it difficult to obtain decisions and resolve disputes.

New organizational functions are needed to address the workstation environment. Some people have proposed that a new corporate function be established to manage information, in the same way that the controller manages other resources. The person who heads this function is called the chief information officer. Many organizations attempt to accomplish workstation management either through the data processing department or an oversight committee. Either approach will work, but a committee is recommended because it provides greater involvement for the operational units in an organization.

One suggested committee approach involves a *Business Systems Planning* (BSP) committee. The chairman of the BSP committee should be the president or the chief executive officer of the organization, except in the case of very large organizations. The committee is comprised of the senior operational officer of the organization, for example, division heads, corporate comptroller, administrative vice president, data administrator, etc. It meets approximately once each month to establish overall direction and priorities for the organization in data processing matters.

The agenda for the BSP committee would be established by the individual members of the committee. Because they represent all of the operating units, they can establish information systems policies, work projects, and budgets for the company. The committee listens to the data processing needs for all of the business activities, and then establishes a priority budget and schedule for those projects. This group can approve workstation support projects.

Each approved project must have a sponsor. The sponsor can be anyone in the organization who has a vested interest in the success of the project. The sponsor is responsible for the funding and completion of the project. Obviously, when an individual is appointed a sponsor, the funding necessary to accomplish that task goes with the sponsorship. The sponsor can contract the work in-house to the central data processing function, allocate it among various organizational units, or contract it to an outside vendor. The decision of which to use is left to the sponsor.

The sponsor is also responsible for the quality of the project being developed. This means that the sponsor should establish the appropriate quality control mechanisms to ensure that the project is adequately completed. Many sponsors form a review board comprised of various users to oversee the quality of the sponsor's project.

Step 3: Monitor Progress Against The Plan. The quality control mechanisms established by the sponsor (or someone similar) are the methods used to monitor progress. The approved data processing projects should be consistent with the plan. The review board (or equivalent quality control mechanism) then reviews the plan to ensure that the approved project is accomplished in accordance with it, and meets the objective of it. If a project is inconsistent with the plan, the BSP committee should change the long-range plan.

Step 4: Reward Individuals Who Accomplish the Plan's Objectives. People do what they are rewarded for. It is immaterial how the reward system is designed, it is the rewards actually given that count. If management wants specific objectives accomplished, and they reward individuals for accomplishing those objectives, it is highly probable that they will be accomplished. On the other hand, if management says it wants certain objectives accomplished, but rewards are actually based on other criteria, it is highly probable that the objectives that meet the other criteria will be accomplished. For example, if management says it wants quality, but rewards on schedule and budget, then projects will be completed within budget and on schedule, regardless of the level of quality of those projects.

Chapter 11 included a discussion of the types of rewards, other than financial, which are effective. However, the prerequisite to rewarding is establishing a means to determine whether or not the desired objectives have been accomplished. It is important that the reward system be tied to actual measurable performance.

IMPEDIMENTS AND
COUNTERSTRATEGIES TO USING THE NEW METHODS

Like the failure to achieve quality, the failure to use the new methods is directly related to personal priorities. If it is important to you to use workstations, they will be used. On the other hand, if other items continually take a higher priority, then the new methods will fall into disuse.

There are two major impediments undermining the use of the new workstation methods. The first is an inadequate system of rewards. Rewards make the world go around. Whatever is rewarded is what is done. Without rewards, there is little motivation to begin workstation processing. In some instances, rewards are given to others for not using the workstation. This can be devastating, because it discloses management's true intent.

The counterstrategy is to tie rewards to desired usage. It is easy to say that the reward system should be tied to workstation usage, but difficult to implement. If managers get the desired results without using workstations, it is difficult to withhold rewards, because the method used is not the desired method. Management is normally rewarded on results, not methods. Thus, it is important to demonstrate increased productivity through workstation usage, as well as establishing the reward system.

The other is the fear of failure. People feel comfortable continuing those practices which have caused them to be successful. Very few managers owe their success to the use of workstations. Therefore, a manager must deviate from a personal pattern of success when using a workstation. This poses the threat not only of the inability to use the new technology, but also the threat to personal success.

The counterstrategy is to establish a support structure. An effective support system must be put in place to help assure managers that they will not fail when using the workstation. Clearly established benefits, together with a support structure that helps make each manager successful, are essential to the effective use of the new technology. People are much more willing to try something new when they are convinced their probability of being successful with it is very high.

SELF-ASSESSMENT CHECKLIST

You should continually assess the methods by which you do work. This is an important part of increasing one's personal productivity. It also provides a vehicle for determining areas where productivity improvements are possible.

Self-assessment is one of management's control responsibilities. Figure 12-3 is a self-assessment checklist for evaluating how well the new methods are being used. This checklist is constructed so that "yes" responses indicate good workstation practices, and "no" responses represent potential areas for personal improvement.

Item	Response			
	Yes	No	N/A	Comments
1. Has senior management determined what new methods they want managers to utilize?				
2. Are managerial workstations one of those new methods?				
3. Have the productivity benefits associated with those new methods been identified?				
4. Are the managerial reward systems tied to using the new methods?				
5. Have appropriate technical support mechanisms been established to assist managers in using the new methods?				
6. Are workstations included in the data processing long-range plan?				
7. Do managers understand how workstation usage fits into the organization's long-range data processing plan?				
8. Is the organizational structure consistent with that long-range data processing plan?				
9. Have quality control mechanisms been established to monitor progress of implementing the plan?				
10. Is the quality control process in place and working?				
11. Can progress of individual managers be tracked against that plan (i.e., the manager's specific work objectives)?				
12. Have managerial workstation user groups been established to provide mutual support among managers?				

13. Has a hot line been established so that managers can get quick answers if they should have problems with the workstation?				
14. Are managers who abandon workstations or utilize them ineffectively subject to reduced rewards compared to the managers who effectively use workstations?				
15. Has a senior-level management planning committee (e.g., a Business System Planning committee) been established to oversee the direction and priority of data processing projects?				

Fig. 12-3. The new methods self-assessment checklist.

WORKSTATION RULE OF THUMB
If managers viewed themselves as entrepreneurs, they would recognize the importance of using new methods in order to remain competitive in the marketplace.

Chapter 13

Evaluating
Effectiveness

*When you work for a long time in an environment, it is difficult
to see the flaws. You should step back periodically and evaluate
whether or not the workstation is improving your on-the-job performance.*

Each of the ten actions in the book contained assessment information. This
was designed to help you evaluate whether or not you had performed the action correctly. However, this assessment was a low-level, item-by-item assessment. It is possible that each item would be correct, and yet you might be
dissatisfied with the total action. For example, in building an automobile, each
part of the engine might be built according to specifications, but, when put
together, the engine does not work. The person building each part would be
happy, but the buyer would not be.

This chapter provides a plan of action to improve areas in which your assessment is unsatisfactory to you. The improvement programs are subjective,
but give you goals to attempt to achieve and methods for achieving them.

WORKSTATION SELF-ASSESSMENT METHODS

There are four general methods of evaluating an activity such as a workstation. The self-assessment method is recommended here because it is a quantitative method. It focuses attention on numbers, rather than opinions,
judgments, or low-level attributes.

Method 1: Judgment. The judgmental evaluation method is one in which "experts" evaluate the workstation activity. Under this approach, the appraisal group must provide the needed expertise, in order to develop an opinion relating to the assessment objectives. The experts normally develop the opinion by comparing the workstation function (or whatever is being judged) against their personal opinion and experience. In some instances, a "model" is used as the criteria against which the evaluation is made. For example, the assessment team will predetermine what the ideal workstation environment should be, and then compare what they actually see against that ideal.

The judgmental opinion is only as good as the judges. If they are highly respected and know their field, the assessment can be outstanding. On the other hand, judgment is difficult to substantiate and frequently results in second-guessing by the individuals judged or by others. Too often, everyone thinks they are a better judge than the judge.

Method 2: Attributes. Attributes are criteria used to evaluate performance. If the item being evaluated possesses those attributes, it is given a positive evaluation, but, if the attributes are missing, the assessment is negative. In this method, the definition of the attributes is the key to assessment.

An example will demonstrate the difference between judgment and attribute assessment. In a classroom situation, the attributes would be the individual skills or activities that an individual must master. Assume that there were ten skills to be mastered. The assessment would then determine whether or not the individual had mastered those ten skills, and would report what skills had been mastered and what had not. If the same classroom used judgment assessment, the instructor would use whatever means they desired to evaluate the student, and then provide a grade based on the instructor's assessment. Judgment and attribute assessment, however, are not mutually exclusive methods.

The attribute assessment method is normally noncontroversial after the attributes have been identified and agreed upon. The assessment team conducts whatever investigation is necessary to determine whether or not the specific attributes are present. For this method, the assessment team needs only sufficient skills to be able to identify whether or not the desired attributes are present. The assessment team does not make a judgment regarding the desirability of the attributes, just the presence or absence of those attributes.

This book has made extensive use of the attribute approach. The managerial workstation attributes described in this book include:

- Managerial strategies for workstations.
- Workstation survival methods. If these rules have been followed, the desirable attributes will be present.
- Self-assessment checklists included at the end of the survival chapters. These checklists provide very detailed criteria that can be used by an assessment team.

The attributes method is the easiest assessment method to perform. It is of greatest value in the early days of using a new technology, because it is generally considered to be a fair method. It also provides the group being assessed with the opportunity to challenge or discuss the attributes. It is very specific about what must be done to improve the results of the next assessment.

Method 3: Qualitative Method. This method requires the assessment team to define workstation performance in one of a group of evaluative terms. For example, the classroom method of assigning letter grades could be used, or a simpler method stating that the assessment is either fully satisfactory, satisfactory, or less than satisfactory.

The qualitative method forces the assessment team to categorize the results of the assessment, comparing them to previous reviews. For example, if the workstation activities were judged less than satisfactory a year ago, and satisfactory today, it would be obvious that performance had improved.

The judgmental method is unstructured, and thus might describe a situation in narrative terms. The attribute method states what is and is not present, but does not draw an opinion about the desirability of the present or missing attributes. The qualitative method forces the reviewers to come up with a distinct opinion regarding performance.

The qualitative method is frequently used in conjunction with one of the other three methods. One of these methods is followed, and at the end, the assessment team summarizes their work with a qualitative assessment, and explains how that qualitative assessment was derived.

Method 4: Quantitative Method. The quantitative method produces a numerical value from the assessment. The numerical value represents the assessment, but might need interpretation. The numerical number is normally representative of a raw score, to be evaluated by someone knowledgeable in the area being assessed.

Most professional assessments are quantitative. For example, accountants evaluate an organization quantitatively, in terms of net profit, gross profit, and inventory turnover. Doctors evaluate patients in terms of blood pressure, temperature, weight and height. Engineers evaluate structures in terms of resistance, stress, and load factors. It is not unrealistic, then, that workstation assessment produces numerical values from the assessment process.

RECOMMENDED EVALUATION METHOD

The installation and operation of your workstation revolves around ten actions. These actions, described in Chapters 3 through 12, are used as the basis for evaluating your installed workstation. Each action was designed to describe an event, which, if it occurred effectively, would result in productive workstation processing.

At this point, you should have read the actions and attempted to accomplish them. In performing each action, you were asked to perform some detailed self-assessments regarding implementing the action. These self-assessments were designed primarily to ensure that you implemented the action correctly. If you followed those procedures, you would have performed quality control over implementing that action.

The self-assessment you will now be going through is equivalent to the quality assurance function. You have controlled each of the actions, and now you are trying to evaluate whether the sum of those steps actually achieve the desired results. This assessment will help you determine whether or not you have been successful by quantitatively evaluating the results that you should have achieved from performing the actions. For example, the first action was to use management approaches to implement the workstation. The result of that action should be an outstanding workstation installed in your office.

Each of the ten actions has been converted into the expected result for the self-assessment process. Figure 13-1 lists the ten expected results from the ten actions described in this book. If you are uncertain precisely what that result means, you should reread the appropriate chapter. The item number used corresponds to the action number presented in Chapters 3 through 12. For each of the actions, give your assessment of how well you have achieved that result. The seven variations of assessment are as follows:

- Evaluation 1 (very poor): The action resulted in an activity which is not useful, or not functional.
- Evaluation 2 (poor): The result permits some work to be done, but it cannot be relied upon.
- Evaluation 3 (below average): Work can be performed, but it either contains more than expected defects, or is too complex.
- Evaluation 4 (average): The objective for this area has been met, but just barely.
- Evaluation 5 (above average): The objective has been implemented in a fully satisfactory manner in all aspects.
- Evaluation 6 (superior): Performance in this area is above expectations.
- Evaluation 7 (outstanding): The system can be viewed as fantastic, beyond belief.

The words attached to the seven-point assessment scale merely attempt to differentiate degrees of satisfaction. The fourth level of assessment is the norm. Below that is less than what was expected, and above it means the results exceeded expectations.

In making this evaluation, refer to the self-assessment checklists in the appropriate chapter. The answers that you got to those questions will be helpful in developing this evaluation. Remember, however, that although it is meant to be subjective, it is based on the experiences that you are having with your workstation. This self-assessment should be performed periodically, probably every six months for the first two years of workstation installation, and then annually after that.

Number	Item (expected results from the ten proposed actions)	Evaluation						
		Very poor 1	Poor 2	Bel. Avg. 3	Aver-age 4	Above Avg. 5	Super-ior 6	Out-standing 7
1.	The functions and features associated with the workstation have been implemented, and they meet your job responsibility needs. (This does not mean that you can operate them properly but, rather, that the basic features that you need for your job are there.)							
2.	You are able to use the workstation features effectively.							
3.	You have documented procedures which tell you how to utilize your workstation, and when you follow those procedures you can perform the tasks effectively.							
4.	The workstation layout in your office is conducive to the effective use of the workstation, and you are pleased with the way it looks.							
5.	You have available, on the workstation, the data that you need to do your job.							
6.	You have been able to increase your own personal productivity through the use of your workstation.							
7.	In using your workstation, you are able to interface with those individuals/groups necessary to perform your job responsibilities.							
8.	You have identified the technical support groups that you need to assist you, and those groups provide all of the support that you need.							
9.	You have been able to operate your workstation in a defect-free manner.							
10.	You have been able to incorporate the workstation into the performance of your day-to-day activities and now rely at least partially on that workstation for performing your activities.							

Fig. 13-1. Worksheet to evaluate the results of the ten actions.

WHAT DOES THE EVALUATION MEAN?

The self-assessment evaluation you have now completed records your assessment of workstation effectiveness. It will indicate which areas you feel are below your expectations, and which areas exceed your expectations. However, you should not be satisfied with an average rating, but should attempt to move all categories into the outstanding class.

The purpose of the assessment is to form the basis for improvement. Those items receiving the lowest rating are the primary candidates for improvement. You should not be disappointed with initial low ratings, but you should be disappointed if you don't develop action programs to improve those ratings.

Developing a Workstation Improvement Program

The framework for improvement is outlined in the ten chapters describing the ten actions. Those chapters, however, do not provide a goal for measuring improvement. That goal will be established using the results of the self-assessment in Fig. 13-1.

The starting point for the workstation improvement program will be your current assessment of the ten areas. For example, assume that you evaluated item 1 as a three. Item 1 is related to how well the workstation has been installed. Assume, further, that you are currently dissatisfied with your workstation capabilities, and want some improvement. You might decide that you would like a workstation that slightly exceeded your expectations, so that if you got the workstation you want, you might evaluate it as a five. Based on this logic, then, your workstation improvement program would set a goal of improving your evaluation of the implemented workstation from a three to a five.

A sample workstation improvement program is illustrated in Fig. 13-2. As a result of the above discussion, you will see on Fig. 13-2 that the improvement goal for item 1 is to move from a three to a five. The figure shows a bar going from the three assessment range to the five assessment range. The X in the bar represents where you now are, and the Y in the bar represents where you want to go. Figure 13-2 has been completed for all ten items, showing hypothetical improvements. However, note that the improvement programs will not address items 3 and 4.

The action program that you establish should be designed to help in the areas where improvement is indicated. These action programs should be developed by evaluating your workstation goals, and the material in the appropriate chapter. It is good to document those improvement programs.

At your next assessment period, you will go back and make your own assessment, to indicate how successful you have been in accomplishing your goal. If you have accomplished your goal and achieved the desired improved assessment, you should be pleased. If you have only partially achieved the goal, you should rededicate yourself to improvement in that area. If you have achieved

Number	Item (Expected Proposed Actions)	Evaluation						
		Very Poor 1	Poor 2	Below Average 3	Average 4	Above Average 5	Superior 6	Outstanding 7
1.	The functions and features associated with the workstation have been implemented, and they meet your job responsibility needs. (This does not mean that you can operate them properly but, rather, that the basic features that you need for your job are there.)			X		Y		
2.	You are able to use the workstation features effectively.				X	Y		
3.	You have documented procedures which tell you how to utilize your workstation, and when you follow those procedures you can perform the tasks effectively.				X-Y			
4.	The workstation layout in your office is conducive to the effective use of the workstation, and you are pleased with the way it looks.				X-Y			
5.	You have available, on the workstation, the data that you need to do your job.		X				Y	
6.	You have been able to increase your own personal productivity through the use of your workstation.						X	Y
7.	In using your workstation, you are able to interface with those individuals/groups necessary to perform your job responsibilities.			X	Y			
8.	You have identified the technical support groups that you need to assist you, and those groups provide all of the support that you need.		X	Y				
9.	You have been able to operate your workstation in a defect-free manner.				X			Y
10.	You have been able to incorporate the workstation into the performance of your day-to-day activities and now rely at least partially on that workstation for performing your activities.			X	Y			

Fig. 13-2. An example of a workstation evaluation.

your goal, you might want to set a new goal for the next period and work toward an even better improvement.

Properly conducted, these assessments provide very valuable information. You are responsible for your workstation process. The fully satisfied workstation user will continually be taking action to improve the workstation process. The result of these improvements will be increased satisfaction with your workstation, and increased personal productivity.

WORKSTATION RULE OF THUMB
There is no greater finale to installing a workstation system than the words: "It is done." An independent evaluator can assess whether this is so, and if not, why.

Appendix

Problem Diagnosis

Whatever can go wrong with your workstation will go wrong. It is not a question of whether you will have problems but, rather, a question of how you deal with them. Workstation users who can deal with problems effectively derive greater benefits from the workstation.

A problem is an unexpected event occurring during workstation usage. In some instances, the output will appear erroneous. In other cases, you will not even be able to get the workstation to operate. However, you will probably not experience a problem that someone has not already faced. Therefore, the purpose of this appendix is to help you solve those problems using the combined experiences of other workstation users.

The steps that you should take to resolve workstation problems are:

Step 1: Identify that a problem has occurred. You should be continually alert to the operations and results produced by your workstation. When you believe something is malfunctioning, you have identified a problem. Some of these are obvious, like processing stopping in the middle of operations, while other problems are more subtle, for example, the output is inconsistent with what you expected.

Step 2: Document the problem attributes. You should attempt to record as many attributes of the problem as you can. Note what instruction you were using, what sequence of events led up to the problem, what input was being processed, what output was produced, what diagnostic message was displayed or printed, and so forth. In large installations, they have special forms for recording these attributes of problems. However, there is no need to be that formal at a workstation. All you need to do is carefully note the events that led up to the problem, and the status of processing at the time the problem was identified.

Step 3: Scan the problems in this appendix, and select the most appropriate one. This appendix identifies 38 problems associated with workstation processing. You should become familiar with the titles of these problems, and, if the titles are not self-explanatory, read the descriptions associated with them. From this list, select the problem that most closely represents the one you identified in Step 1.

Step 4: Turn to the page identifying that problem. First, identify that the problem description is representative of the problem you identified in Step 1. Then, determine that you have collected all of the recommended data, as suggested in the problem diagnosis worksheet. If you haven't gathered all of the information and it is still available, record it.

Step 5: Try the quick fix approach. From the "quick fix approach" section, try the procedure recommended there. If it is successful in resolving the problem, go to Step 7. If it doesn't work, perform the next step.

Step 6: Take alternate action if the quick fix does not work. Try the alternate actions recommended on a diagnostic problem program. If these alternate approaches work, go to the next step. If they do not work, there are two possibilities. First, the problem that you have selected might not be the correct problem to use in this case. Study it again, try to select another problem, and select the diagnostic program for that problem. This would require repeating several of the above steps. If you feel you have the right problem, but the quick fix approach and the alternative actions did not work, then contact the person listed in the diagnostic program for help.

Step 7: Develop a long-term solution. To complete this step you will have to make a judgment. If the problem was a minor one, for example, incorrect input, you might decide that additional action is unnecessary. However, if the problem appears to be one that would reoccur without action, then complete the problem solution action included at the bottom of the diagnostic program.

The problems addressed in this appendix in the order in which they appear, are:

1: Abnormal termination
2: Backup data needed but not available
3: Changing use of function keys
4: Communication lines out
5: Difficult-to-use software
6: Error message received
7: Error message unclear
8: Errors in output
9: Excessive computer resources
10: Excessive time to recover
11: Files destroyed
12: Files lost
13: Inadequate computer resources
14: Incompatible file structure
15: Input data incomplete
16: Input data lost
17: Input data wrong

18: Maintaining redundant data
19: Needed project/information delayed
20: Needed technical help unavailable
21: Needed technical help unknown
22: No one accepts responsibility for problem
23: Operating language difficult to understand
24: Operating results cannot be reproduced
25: Operating system difficult to use
26: Out-of-balance reports
27: Output data inaccurate

28: Output data incomplete
29: Output data lost
30: Output headings not understood
31: Power failure
32: Problem identification difficulty
33: Processing incomplete
34: Processing incorrect
35: Purchased application needs modification
36: Software lockup
37: Software performs differently than documentation indicates
38: Workstation outputs cannot be reconciled to corporate outputs

PROBLEM DIAGNOSTIC PROGRAM NUMBER 1

PROBLEM NAME Abnormal termination   SEVERITY Medium

PROBLEM DESCRIPTION Processing stops for a reason identified by the workstation processing capability.

DATA TO COLLECT Collect type of abnormal termination, and status of program and files at point of termination.

QUICK FIX APPROACH Identify the event that caused the abnormal termination, for example, incorrect input, and eliminate that event and continue processing.

ACTION IF QUICK FIX DOES NOT WORK Identify the type of action required by the vendor of the software, take that action, and continue processing.

BEST PERSON(S) TO CALL FOR HELP Someone knowledgeable with software package.

PROBLEM SOLUTION Identify the root cause of the abnormal termination, for example, insufficient disk space, and change procedures so that that cause will be significantly reduced or eliminated.

154

PROBLEM DIAGNOSTIC PROGRAM NUMBER 2

PROBLEM NAME Backup data needed but not available   SEVERITY High

PROBLEM DESCRIPTION   You want to use backup data to reprocess or confirm processing
and the needed backup data is no longer available.

DATA TO COLLECT   Collect type of backup data needed, backup data available, and
backup procedures.

QUICK FIX APPROACH   No quick fix available.

ACTION IF QUICK FIX DOES NOT WORK   If backup data is available for a previous period,
and the events between that period and the time frame desired are available, then
processing can be performed from the date of the existing backup to the point where
the backup data is needed.

BEST PERSON(S) TO CALL FOR HELP   Workstation development group.

PROBLEM SOLUTION   Develop procedures which will ensure availability of backup
data when needed.

PROBLEM DIAGNOSTIC PROGRAM NUMBER 3

PROBLEM NAME Changing use of function keys   SEVERITY Medium

PROBLEM DESCRIPTION   The action that needs to be performed is directed toward a
specific function key in one part of processing, and then later in processing
to do that exact same action requires the use of another function key. For example,
to escape out of processing at one time takes function key 1, and at a later time,
is function key 9.

DATA TO COLLECT   Collect function key usage by screen (to note at what point
function key functions change.)

QUICK FIX APPROACH   Write detailed procedures to follow to prompt you on what function
keys you should use.

ACTION IF QUICK FIX DOES NOT WORK   Assure that if you use the wrong function key
that the action performed will cause you to recognize that a wrong function key
has been depressed. At that point, take corrective action to continue processing
correctly.

BEST PERSON(S) TO CALL FOR HELP   Vendor/technical support group.

PROBLEM SOLUTION   To standardize the use of function keys throughout single
software systems, and preferably through all systems used at a workstation.

155

PROBLEM NAME___Communication lines out_____ SEVERITY_Medium___

PROBLEM DESCRIPTION The communication lines used to receive and transmit data to
other workstations/facilities are out of use due to problems with the communication
lines.

DATA TO COLLECT Collect which communication lines are down, when communication
lines will be returned to usage, and alternative methods for transmitting data.

QUICK FIX APPROACH Receive/transmit data by other means. For example, messenger.

ACTION IF QUICK FIX DOES NOT WORK Alternatives include:

1. Waiting until communication lines are back in order and continuing processing
   at that point in time.
2. Using other facilities to receive/communicate data, for example, another
   workstation might be operational and the data needed can be received/
   transmitted to that workstation.

BEST PERSON(S) TO CALL FOR HELP Director of communications.

PROBLEM SOLUTION Develop backup procedures that will assure processing can
occur within the desired time frame.

PROBLEM NAME Difficult-to-use software   SEVERITY Low

PROBLEM DESCRIPTION
The methods that are required to use the features of a software system are complex/extensive enough to make using the software difficult.

DATA TO COLLECT
Collect current operating instructions; note areas of difficult processing; and note procedures that have to be followed (which are understandable to you).

QUICK FIX APPROACH
Develop detailed step-by-step procedures which assure that the software can be used correctly.

ACTION IF QUICK FIX DOES NOT WORK
Request someone knowledgeable with the software to assist you in performing it to determine whether there is an easier way of operation.

BEST PERSON(S) TO CALL FOR HELP
Someone knowledgeable with software package.

PROBLEM SOLUTION
Have individuals knowledgeable with software develop simpler procedures to operate the software to reduce the potential problems .

PROBLEM NAME Error message received   SEVERITY Medium

PROBLEM DESCRIPTION
Processing continued through to conclusion, but one or more error message was produced during processing.

DATA TO COLLECT
Collect name/number of error message, what error message means, and what must be done in order to correct problem.

QUICK FIX APPROACH
Study the problem noted in the error message, take corrective action before using processing results.

ACTION IF QUICK FIX DOES NOT WORK
Use processing results but note the potential problem with those results.

BEST PERSON(S) TO CALL FOR HELP
Someone knowledgeable with software package.

PROBLEM SOLUTION
Identify the root cause of the error message and adjust procedures in order to reduce or eliminate the cause of that problem.

157

PROBLEM NAME Error message unclear   SEVERITY Medium

PROBLEM DESCRIPTION An error message is produced by the software package, but the intent of the message and/or the action to take is unclear.

DATA TO COLLECT Collect name/number of error message, description of error message, what must be done in order to overcome problem, and who must be contacted to identify the true meaning of the error message.

QUICK FIX APPROACH Call someone knowledgeable about the software and ask them what action you need to take based on the error message.

ACTION IF QUICK FIX DOES NOT WORK Alternatives include:

1. Rerunning the software to determine whether the error message will reoccur.
2. Eliminate the event that caused the error message and process without that event.
3. Call the software package vendor hot line if one is available to determine what action to take.

BEST PERSON(S) TO CALL FOR HELP Software vendor/knowledgeable user of software.

PROBLEM SOLUTION Develop more definitive descriptions of the error message and action to be taken on those messages.

158

PROBLEM DIAGNOSTIC PROGRAM NUMBER 8___

PROBLEM NAME Errors in output _____ SEVERITY High _____

PROBLEM DESCRIPTION The output does not contain the correct data. The incorrect information may be descriptions, report values, report headings, or the location of data on the report.

DATA TO COLLECT Collect output with errors on it, and description of program and processing at time error occurred.

QUICK FIX APPROACH Examine the parameter that established the report, and correct those parameters if incorrect.

ACTION IF QUICK FIX DOES NOT WORK Other actions that can be taken to correct reports include:

1. Manually correcting improper printed data.
2. Correct input if there are errors in input.
3. Explain on the report the source of the error and how to use it.

BEST PERSON(S) TO CALL FOR HELP Someone familiar with the software in question.

PROBLEM SOLUTION Correct the report parameters and/or operating procedures until the correct report can be produced.

PROBLEM DIAGNOSTIC PROGRAM NUMBER 9

PROBLEM NAME Excessive computer resources   SEVERITY Low

| PROBLEM DESCRIPTION | The workstation sits idle during large segments of the work day. |

| DATA TO COLLECT | Collect amount of time used for processing, and resources consumed by job (will end up in a ranking of jobs by resources consumed). |

| QUICK FIX APPROACH | Make workstation available to others during periods when you will be away from your office. |

| ACTION IF QUICK FIX DOES NOT WORK | Move workstation to common area so several people can use the same workstation. |

| BEST PERSON(S) TO CALL FOR HELP | Individual/group who selected workstation resources. |

| PROBLEM SOLUTION | Utilize the workstation more in your day-to-day work. |

PROBLEM DIAGNOSTIC PROGRAM NUMBER 10

PROBLEM NAME Excessive time to recover   SEVERITY Medium

| PROBLEM DESCRIPTION | The amount of time required to perform a recovery is almost more than the benefits that will be derived from making the recovery. In addition, the recovery time may be so long that the needed processing will not be available on a timely basis. |

| DATA TO COLLECT | Collect purpose for recovery, condition surrounding failure that caused recovery, procedures evoked during recovery, and resources expended by recovery procedure (if possible). |

| QUICK FIX APPROACH | None. |

| ACTION IF QUICK FIX DOES NOT WORK | Obtain assistance of other people/other workstations in an effort to reduce the amount of time required for recovery. |

| BEST PERSON(S) TO CALL FOR HELP | Workstation development group. |

| PROBLEM SOLUTION | The checkpoint and points of data backup should be established so that the recovery periods are not excessive. Note that this is usually a tradeoff between the time spent preparing for recovery and the ease at which recovery can occur if it is needed. |

160

PROBLEM NAME Files destroyed   SEVERITY High

PROBLEM DESCRIPTION	Files needed for future processing were destroyed through hardware/ software failure or human failure.

DATA TO COLLECT Collect name and content of file, backup files for the destroyed file; and procedures for reconstructing destroyed file.

QUICK FIX APPROACH Rerun processing logic to reproduce output.

ACTION IF QUICK FIX DOES NOT WORK The following alternatives can be used to recreate lost files:

1. Use backup file as source to recreate missing file.
2. Request file from other user, if data is available.
3. Manually reconstruct input so that new files can be created.

BEST PERSON(S) TO CALL FOR HELP Owner of input/file.

PROBLEM SOLUTION Develop backup procedures so that files are copied and protected at the point of origin.

PROBLEM NAME Files lost   SEVERITY High

| PROBLEM DESCRIPTION | Files are stored within the workstation disk storage, but are not accessible through normal processing. |

DATA TO COLLECT — Collect name of lost file, content of lost file, backup for file if available; and original input data if backup file is not available.

QUICK FIX APPROACH — Use operating system recovery routines to recover data/file.

ACTION IF QUICK FIX DOES NOT WORK — If quick fix does not work, collect original input data and reconstruct lost file. This may require extensive processing to go through all of the actions necessary to reconstruct the lost file.

BEST PERSON(S) TO CALL FOR HELP — Workstation technical expert.

PROBLEM SOLUTION — Develop procedures for workstation user to recover lost files. In addition, appropriate backup procedures should be invoked to ensure the information is available if the lost file cannot be retrieved.

PROBLEM NAME ___Inadequate computer resources___ SEVERITY _Medium_

PROBLEM DESCRIPTION   There are inadequate processing resources to perform the desired work. The inadequate resources can be over an extended period of time, for example, a work day, or it can be for a specific period of time, for example, 9 to 10 in the morning, when specific tasks such as a needed daily report must be prepared.

DATA TO COLLECT   Jobs run in time frame in which inadequate resources were available, and jobs needed to be run in that time frame, which could not be because of inadequate resources. Time estimate for the job not run is also desirable.

QUICK FIX APPROACH   Get a second workstation, or give the work to another individual to perform.

ACTION IF QUICK FIX DOES NOT WORK   Attempt to get input earlier so job can start earlier or extend working hours.

BEST PERSON(S) TO CALL FOR HELP   Individual/group who selected workstation resources.

PROBLEM SOLUTION   Obtain a workstation with more processing capabilities, and/or input/output capabilities.

PROBLEM NAME Incompatible file structures   SEVERITY Medium

PROBLEM DESCRIPTION   Data produced by one system cannot be used by another system because it is incompatible. It might be incompatible because of record size, field size, number of variables in the data, or other data characteristics which are inconsistent between the two systems.

DATA TO COLLECT   Collect names of incompatible files, data included on incompatible files, nature of incompatibility (i.e., any error messages), and programs processing files.

QUICK FIX APPROACH   Have someone write a small data conversion program which will convert data from the original format to the format needed.

ACTION IF QUICK FIX DOES NOT WORK   Determine if the system that produced the incompatible file can perform the type of processing needed to meet your needs.

BEST PERSON(S) TO CALL FOR HELP   Workstation development group.

PROBLEM SOLUTION   File conversion program should be developed and readily available, which will convert files from one structure to another. This assumes that the needed file structures have been determined and will be used repetitively.

164

PROBLEM NAME Input data incomplete   SEVERITY High

| PROBLEM DESCRIPTION |
Either transaction items or parts of transactions are missing.

| DATA TO COLLECT |
Collect information on incomplete input data condition, specific
input data missing, and source of the missing data.

| QUICK FIX APPROACH |
Call owners of data to determine the missing value/transaction
and enter same before processing.

| ACTION IF QUICK FIX DOES NOT WORK |
The following alternative actions can be taken:

1. Run without erroneous data, noting same on output reports.
2. Correct data to a reasonable value and follow up to make final correction later.

| BEST PERSON(S) TO CALL FOR HELP |
Owner of data.

| PROBLEM SOLUTION |
Add control totals which readily identify what is missing from
input transactions.

PROBLEM NAME Input data lost   SEVERITY High

PROBLEM DESCRIPTION
Input that is needed to run computer processing cannot be located.

DATA TO COLLECT
Collect description of lost input data, specifics of what data contained, and source of data.

QUICK FIX APPROACH
Identify the source of the data and ask if it can be replaced. Rerun processing with complete data.

ACTION IF QUICK FIX DOES NOT WORK
The following alternative actions can be taken:

1. Run report with data missing indicating on report what is missing.
2. Simulate data by using transactions which you feel approximate the lost input.
3. Delay processing until input can be found.

BEST PERSON(S) TO CALL FOR HELP
Owners of input data.

PROBLEM SOLUTION
Develop procedures which will track input so that its whereabouts can be readily determined.

PROBLEM DIAGNOSTIC PROGRAM NUMBER 17

PROBLEM NAME Input data wrong   SEVERITY Medium

PROBLEM DESCRIPTION   Errors are identified in the input data. The correct amount
may not be known, but the fact that the data is incorrect is known.

DATA TO COLLECT   Collect conditions defining wrong input data, specifics regarding
what is wrong, and original source of input data.

QUICK FIX APPROACH   Call owners of input to find correct value, make correction and
run data.

ACTION IF QUICK FIX DOES NOT WORK   The following alternative actions can be taken:

1. Run without erroneous data, noting same on output reports.
2. Correct data to a reasonable value and follow up to make final correction later.

BEST PERSON(S) TO CALL FOR HELP   Owner of data.

PROBLEM SOLUTION   Develop data validation procedures which will identify incorrect
source of data problems.

PROBLEM DIAGNOSTIC PROGRAM NUMBER 18

PROBLEM NAME Maintaining redundant data   SEVERITY Low

PROBLEM DESCRIPTION   The workstation collects, enters, and maintains data which is
being maintained at one or more facilities throughout the organization.

DATA TO COLLECT   Identify what data is being maintained redundantly, and who
and where the duplicate data is being maintained.

QUICK FIX APPROACH   Compare data to other sources to ensure its integrity.

ACTION IF QUICK FIX DOES NOT WORK   Ignore redundancy and accept expenditure of
unnecessary costs.

BEST PERSON(S) TO CALL FOR HELP   Data base administrator/person responsible for
corporate data.

PROBLEM SOLUTION   Eliminate redundancy and share data among those needing data.

PROBLEM DIAGNOSTIC PROGRAM NUMBER 19

PROBLEM NAME Needed project/information delayed   SEVERITY Medium

PROBLEM DESCRIPTION Either input and/or processing capability needed but will not be ready on needed date.

DATA TO COLLECT Collect data on what project/information is or will not be available when needed, projected delivery date, and contact point for discussion to change delivery date.

QUICK FIX APPROACH Use alternative means of processing.

ACTION IF QUICK FIX DOES NOT WORK Anticipate potential problem and arrange to have more resources allocated to permit needed data/processing capability to be available when needed.

BEST PERSON(S) TO CALL FOR HELP Person in charge of producing needed resource.

PROBLEM SOLUTION Better planning, scheduling, and project management systems.

PROBLEM DIAGNOSTIC PROGRAM NUMBER 20

PROBLEM NAME Needed technical help unavailable   SEVERITY Medium

PROBLEM DESCRIPTION When problems occur you are unable to contact the appropriate individual at the time you need that individual to help you with a processing problem.

DATA TO COLLECT Collect description of condition where help was needed, and individual sources of technical help or unavailable, and individual to contact to remedy the situation.

QUICK FIX APPROACH Contact a knowledgeable user of the facility to ask what needs to be done.

ACTION IF QUICK FIX DOES NOT WORK Contact the vendor or someone in the central data processing group to ask for help.

BEST PERSON(S) TO CALL FOR HELP Workstation development group.

PROBLEM SOLUTION Establish a hot line which is staffed during normal working hours to ensure that someone will be available when needed.

PROBLEM DIAGNOSTIC PROGRAM NUMBER 21

PROBLEM NAME   Needed technical help unknown   SEVERITY High

PROBLEM DESCRIPTION   A problem occurs during workstation processing for which you
do not know the solution, and do not know who to contact in order to find the solution
to the problem.

DATA TO COLLECT   Collect description of situation where help was needed but
source of help was unknown, and individual to contact or remedy the situation.

QUICK FIX APPROACH   Notify workstation development group and ask them to advise who
to contact.

ACTION IF QUICK FIX DOES NOT WORK   Contact other users and/or vendors of capabilities,
asking them if they can provide needed assistance, or if they know who can provide
that needed assistance.

BEST PERSON(S) TO CALL FOR HELP   Workstation development group.

PROBLEM SOLUTION   Develop a list of contacts for technical problems by type, and
make that available to all workstation users. As new situations occur, extend the
list.

169

PROBLEM DIAGNOSTIC PROGRAM NUMBER 22

PROBLEM NAME No one accepts responsibility for problem SEVERITY Medium

PROBLEM DESCRIPTION Problem is between products produced by different vendors and none will accept responsibility for looking and correcting the problem. For example, data sent from one program might not be acceptable by another, and both vendors claim the other is at fault.

DATA TO COLLECT Collect description of condition for which no one accepts responsibility, name of vendor/parties involved, the name of the person to contact to remedy situation.

QUICK FIX APPROACH Pay one or the other vendor extra money to find and fix the problem.

ACTION IF QUICK FIX DOES NOT WORK Alternatives include:

1. Threatening not to deal with vendors unless they accept responsibility for problems.
2. Write interface program.
3. Call on technical experts to assist in solving problem.

BEST PERSON(S) TO CALL FOR HELP Individual responsible for purchasing/contracting workstation facilities.

PROBLEM SOLUTION Incorporate into acquisition contracts who will be responsible for tracing down problems.

170

PROBLEM NAME Operating language difficult to   SEVERITY High
                     understand

PROBLEM DESCRIPTION	The system documentation/system screens use language and terms which are either incomprehensible or difficult to understand.

DATA TO COLLECT	Collect name of operating system, situation in which you are having problems, operating conditions at that time including which programs were run and indications of problems, and who to contact to remedy the situation.

QUICK FIX APPROACH	Develop detailed procedures which will lead you to the right conclusion without needing to understand the language/terms used by the software package.

ACTION IF QUICK FIX DOES NOT WORK	Contact someone knowledgeable of the software package and get description of the terms used by the software package.

BEST PERSON(S) TO CALL FOR HELP	Workstation development group.

PROBLEM SOLUTION	Develop a workstation glossary of terms so that the user of the workstation can refer to that glossary to understand the meaning of any term used in normal processing.

PROBLEM NAME Operating results cannot be reproduced   SEVERITY High

---

PROBLEM DESCRIPTION   The results of operation cannot be reproduced to show how those particular results were obtained. For example, someone might question the correctness or completeness of output, and you need to substantiate how those results were obtained.

DATA TO COLLECT   Collect original results and attempt for reproduction of results; show differences between two processing runs; record the best you can what you did in each operating situation.

QUICK FIX APPROACH   None.

ACTION IF QUICK FIX DOES NOT WORK   Experiment with reprocessing the data, attempting to duplicate how they were first processed, in order to determine through experimentation how the results were produced. This preassumes that the input transactions can be reconstructed.

BEST PERSON(S) TO CALL FOR HELP   Workstation development group.

PROBLEM SOLUTION   Audit trails must be included throughout processing so that a trail is left showing how the specific processing results were obtained. This is particularly important on all critical data produced from workstation processing.

PROBLEM NAME Operating system difficult to use   SEVERITY Low

PROBLEM DESCRIPTION The operating system features are difficult to understand/use, making the workstation process cumbersome or complex for the user.

DATA TO COLLECT Indicate operating situation for which you are having trouble; indicate program and operation, data file used, any condition of problem including parts of manual which are unclear, and who to contact for assistance.

QUICK FIX APPROACH Obtain some instruction on how to use the operating system.

ACTION IF QUICK FIX DOES NOT WORK Develop step-by-step procedures which clearly explain all of the steps that must be done for the mainline processing tasks.

BEST PERSON(S) TO CALL FOR HELP Workstation development group.

PROBLEM SOLUTION The development group should develop methods and procedures which will require lesser skills to use the operating system. If this is not practical, then either more instructions and/or more detailed operating procedures should be prepared.

PROBLEM NAME Out-of-balance reports   SEVERITY High

PROBLEM DESCRIPTION Either vertical columns do not add correctly, or equal a predetermined control amount, or the horizontal cross-checking is out of balance with
the vertical totals.

DATA TO COLLECT Collect information for documenting the out-of-balance reports;
indicate what program and features were being used to produce report; list input
conditions.

QUICK FIX APPROACH Validate the correctness of the individual items, and then manually
develop the totals.

ACTION IF QUICK FIX DOES NOT WORK If the report does not agree with a predetermined
control total, validate that the input is correct and complete. If the mathematical
computations are incorrect, then reprocess the calculation following carefully the
directions provided by the software vendor.

BEST PERSON(S) TO CALL FOR HELP Someone familiar with the processing in question.

PROBLEM SOLUTION One of two solutions should work. First, revise procedures to
ensure that the processing steps can be followed precisely. Second, if the software
is defective, have the software fixed.

174

PROBLEM NAME Output data inaccurate   SEVERITY High

PROBLEM DESCRIPTION The information contained on output reports/screens is not correct. The inaccuracy may be noted by yourself, or identified through diagnostic messages.

DATA TO COLLECT Collect information on inaccurate output conditions, name and feature of program used to produce output, and listing of input data.

QUICK FIX APPROACH Correct the input and reprocess the data.

ACTION IF QUICK FIX DOES NOT WORK Make the appropriate corrections to the output report or distribute the output report as is (use terminal screen as is) noting the inaccuracy.

BEST PERSON(S) TO CALL FOR HELP Individual knowledgeable in software system used.

PROBLEM SOLUTION Correct the operating procedures, or the input validation procedures to increase the probability of accurate output.

PROBLEM DIAGNOSTIC PROGRAM NUMBER 28

PROBLEM NAME Output data incomplete   SEVERITY High

PROBLEM DESCRIPTION The reports/screens to be produced were either incompletely developed, or incompletely prepared.

DATA TO COLLECT Collect information describing incomplete output data; define specifically what is missing; document program and features used to produce output data; list input.

QUICK FIX APPROACH Rerun software system using the procedure supplied by the vendor to determine if incomplete output/screens can be created through rerunning.

ACTION IF QUICK FIX DOES NOT WORK If output/screens cannot be produced, consider using available outputs noting what is missing. Should the problem be associated with input, see the actions relating to input.

BEST PERSON(S) TO CALL FOR HELP Individual knowledgeable in software system.

PROBLEM SOLUTION Correct software system/operating procedures so that using them will produce all the desired outputs.

PROBLEM DIAGNOSTIC PROGRAM NUMBER 29

PROBLEM NAME Output data lost _____   SEVERITY Medium ___

PROBLEM DESCRIPTION
Output has been produced/printed/transmitted and is not available or was not received.

DATA TO COLLECT
Collect description of lost output data, specific pieces of data lost, program, file, and features used to produce output, and listing of input.

QUICK FIX APPROACH
Perform processing to produce output again.

ACTION IF QUICK FIX DOES NOT WORK
Output may be located by:

1. Tracing distribution to destination
2. Obtaining backup copies from queue/backup files

BEST PERSON(S) TO CALL FOR HELP
Individual familiar with output distribution.

PROBLEM SOLUTION
Correct procedures to ensure proper dissemination of output.

176

PROBLEM NAME Output headings not understood   SEVERITY Low

PROBLEM DESCRIPTION . Output reports are printed/screens displayed, but you are uncertain as to the meaning of the output headings. This usually occurs because of the cryptic way in which columnar headings/report names are printed.

DATA TO COLLECT   Describe output heading not understood, and program from which the report was produced.

QUICK FIX APPROACH   Refer to the software documentation to determine the full explanation of the report name, columnar heading.

ACTION IF QUICK FIX DOES NOT WORK   Call someone knowledgeable with the output report/ screen to determine the meaning of the report/columnar heading.

BEST PERSON(S) TO CALL FOR HELP   Software development group.

PROBLEM SOLUTION   Change the name of the report/columnar heading. Note that after extensive use with any report this may not be necessary as the user will become familiar with the true meaning of the report/columnar headings.

PROBLEM DIAGNOSTIC PROGRAM NUMBER 31

PROBLEM NAME Power failure   SEVERITY Medium

PROBLEM DESCRIPTION
During process, there is power lossage which either causes processing to malfunction, or power is not available for an extended period of time.

DATA TO COLLECT
Indicate time and length of output failure and conditions that occurred upon trying to restart system; specifically define any problem encountered.

QUICK FIX APPROACH
When power is resumed, validate the integrity of processing and continue processing. Note at these points files may be lost. See the diagnostic program for the lost file problem.

ACTION IF QUICK FIX DOES NOT WORK If power is out for extended times or you are unable to recoup normal processing, consider using other workstations to perform needed tasks.

BEST PERSON(S) TO CALL FOR HELP
Workstation development group.

PROBLEM SOLUTION
Develop backup procedures for workstation users to follow in the event of power outages.

178

PROBLEM NAME Problem identification difficulty   SEVERITY Medium

---

PROBLEM DESCRIPTION
Something does not appear to be correct, and yet the fact that a problem exists is difficult to pinpoint. On the other hand, without increased accurance of the correctness of processing, you may be reluctant to use the results of processing.

DATA TO COLLECT
Collect data that describes the situation in which you are uncomfortable including programs being run, outputs, inputs, processing features, and actions that you took. Use these to work with an expert to verify correctness or incorrectness of processing.

QUICK FIX APPROACH
Perform one or two manual calculations which will indicate whether or not workstation processing is being performed correctly. If the concern is over communication, then confirmation from the recipient may provide the needed assurance.

ACTION IF QUICK FIX DOES NOT WORK
The following alternative actions can be taken:

1. Reprocess input to determine if same outputs are received.
2. Modify input in a controlled manner to measure impact on output.
3. Use test data to test processing.
4. Request assistance from someone familiar with processing.

BEST PERSON(S) TO CALL FOR HELP
Someone familiar with processing in question.

PROBLEM SOLUTION
Validate the correctness of processing using test data or limited transactions. If incorrect processing occurs, trace processing step-by-step to identify problem.

PROBLEM DIAGNOSTIC PROGRAM NUMBER 33

PROBLEM NAME Processing incomplete   SEVERITY High

PROBLEM DESCRIPTION
All of the expected outputs from processing were not produced.

DATA TO COLLECT
Collect information on incomplete processing condition; define files used, input entered into the system, programs and features used in program during processing. Note any special processing actions you took.

QUICK FIX APPROACH
Rerun processing to determine if missing processing is produced.

ACTION IF QUICK FIX DOES NOT WORK
The following alternatives should be considered:

1. Manually develop the missing processing segments.
2. Use alternative processing software if available.

BEST PERSON(S) TO CALL FOR HELP
Someone familiar with processing logic.

PROBLEM SOLUTION
Obtain software and develop procedures which will permit correct processing to occur.

180

PROBLEM NAME Processing incorrect   SEVERITY High

PROBLEM DESCRIPTION
The results of processing are not what was expected based on the defined processing rules.

DATA TO COLLECT
Collect the results of processing, either output or screen displays. Indicate item of incorrect processing; collect input and describe program and features used during processing. Be specific about keys depressed during processing.

QUICK FIX APPROACH
Reread processing procedures and if procedural errors have been made correct them and rerun processing.

ACTION IF QUICK FIX DOES NOT WORK
1. Use processing results but note the errors in processing.
2. Use alternative processing programs if available.

BEST PERSON(S) TO CALL FOR HELP
Someone familiar with processing logic.

PROBLEM SOLUTION
Obtain software and develop procedures which will permit correct processing to occur.

PROBLEM DIAGNOSTIC PROGRAM NUMBER 35

PROBLEM NAME   Purchased application needs modification   SEVERITY Medium

| PROBLEM DESCRIPTION | The desired processing cannot occur unless a purchased application is modified. |

PROBLEM DESCRIPTION   The desired processing cannot occur unless a purchased application is modified.

DATA TO COLLECT   Collect name of purchased application feature/function needed not included in the application and name of vendor.

QUICK FIX APPROACH   Pay vendor to make modification.

ACTION IF QUICK FIX DOES NOT WORK   Alternatives include:

1.   Write interface program to avoid modification.
2.   Modify outputs after produced.
3.   Have internal technicians make modification.

BEST PERSON(S) TO CALL FOR HELP   Someone knowledgeable with product.

PROBLEM SOLUTION   Do not acquire products which fail to meet processing needs. Note this may require the involvement of users in the acquisition process.

PROBLEM DIAGNOSTIC PROGRAM NUMBER 36

PROBLEM NAME Software lockup   SEVERITY Low

PROBLEM DESCRIPTION   During processing, using a software package, processing stops with no message or apparent cause for stoppage.

DATA TO COLLECT   Collect information regarding processing status at time of lockup including program being processed, feature being used, last operating action, files and data being processed at time of lockup.

QUICK FIX APPROACH   Reload program and restart processing from the beginning.

ACTION IF QUICK FIX DOES NOT WORK   Return to a checkpoint, for example, the point where data was backed up, and restart processing from that checkpoint.

BEST PERSON(S) TO CALL FOR HELP   Someone familiar with software package.

PROBLEM SOLUTION   Have technical expert identify the cause of the software lockup and modify procedures accordingly to avoid that condition.

PROBLEM NAME Software performs differently than   SEVERITY Low
documentation indicates

PROBLEM DESCRIPTION

The execution of the software is different than what is expected based upon the documented software specifications. For example, the documentation might indicate that there are two variations of the same report, when in fact there is only one.

DATA TO COLLECT·

Collect documentation for action that software performed differently; collect information illustrating the incorrect processing according to the documentation, and name of vendor/contact to resolve difference with.

QUICK FIX APPROACH

Rely on the execution as opposed to the documentation.

ACTION IF QUICK FIX DOES NOT WORK

If the actual results do not meet your processing needs, then your option is to manually extend the processing to perform those documented features which are not in the executable system.

BEST PERSON(S) TO CALL FOR HELP

Vendor.

PROBLEM SOLUTION

Bring the executable system and the documentation of that system into synchronization so that what the documentation says, the system does.

PROBLEM NAME Workstation outputs cannot be   SEVERITY High
reconciled to corporate outputs

PROBLEM DESCRIPTION
Processing results for a workstation using what appears to be the same data and for the same period produces different output results than that produced by the central processing facility. The difference is normally caused due to misunderstanding about the data or what is included in specific processing periods.

DATA TO COLLECT
Collect outputs that are unreconcilable to corporate outputs; collect inputs used for processing and program/features used for processing. Name of individual responsible for corporate outputs is needed to resolve difference.

QUICK FIX APPROACH
Obtain from the central data processing function the appropriate control total for the period being processed.

ACTION IF QUICK FIX DOES NOT WORK
Indicate on any use of the output data that it has been prepared for planning purposes only, and should not be relied upon as the official corporate results.

BEST PERSON(S) TO CALL FOR HELP
Corporate data base administrator.

PROBLEM SOLUTION
Procedures should be developed that enable workstation users to understand data attributes, and have available a means for reconciling corporate results to workstation-produced results.

184

Index

implementation strategies for, 134
self-assessment checklist for, 142

O

objectives, 26
office efficiency, 62
office layout, 65
  efficiency in, 63, 71
  ensuring adequate, 69, 70
  impediments and counterstrategies to developing, 71
  strategies for, 66
  self-assessment checklist on, 72
operating languages, 171
operations, 172, 173
optical character readers (OCRs), 13
organizational structures, 138
out-of-balance reports, 174
output data, 159, 175, 176, 177, 184

P

paperwork reduction, 3
performance appraisal, 8
personal space requirements, 69
plan of action, development of, 9
power failures, 178
printers, 14
privacy in the office, 68
problem diagnosis, 152-184
problem identification, 179
problem solving, 15
procedures, 49
  development of, 54
  impediments and counterstrategies to development of, 58
  writing up, 57
productivity, 3, 62, 85-98
  achieving personal improvements to, 93
  evaluation of, 28, 31, 32, 86
  impediments and counterstrategies to, 96
  improvement of, 87, 88
  self-assessment checklist for, 97

Q

qualitative method, 146
quality control, 87, 122-132, 140
  implementation strategies for, 125
  process for ensuring, 128-131
  theory of, 124
  self-assessment checklist for, 131
quantitative method, 146
quick-fix approach, 153

R

redundant data, 167
reliable information
  acquisition strategies for, 81
  generation of, 82
  impediments and counterstrategies to acquiring, 82
  sources of, 79, 80, 81
responsibility, 30, 170

rewards system, 134, 141

S

security in the office, 68
self-assessment exercise, 4-6
self-assessment methods, 144
social interaction in office, 65, 92
software, 14, 157, 182, 183
statistical quality control, 124, 126
survival strategies for the workstation, 5, 8
systems modification, 182

T

task baseline, 54
tasks/capabilities matrix, 54-57
technical help, 112-121, 169
  acquisition and use of, 117-119
  impediments and counterstrategies to using, 119
  implementation strategies for, 115
  realistic use of, 112, 114
  self-assessment checklist for, 120
technical support system, 136
technology, 8, 12
training strategies, 37, 39-40, 53, 126
two-line capability, 13

U

uploading, 50, 78, 104
usage baseline, 68
user groups, 137

V

vendor technical staff, 116
vendors, 127

W

word processing, 13
work plan, 26
work-effectiveness principles, 87, 93
workstation
  capabilities of, 13, 21, 44, 54
  components of, 12
  control of, 7, 22, 28
  customization of, 11-22
  definition of, 12
  design and implementation of, 25
  developing improvement program for, 149
  effective use of, 1, 22, 49-60
  equipment requirements for, 69
  experimentation with, 1, 6
  learning curve for, 7
  location for, 61-73
  mastery of, 2, 36, 38, 42
  problems caused by, 6
  pros and cons of, 2
  reliance upon, 8
  self-assessment checklist for, 47, 59
"workstation friendly," 35-48
  impediments and counterstrategies to becoming, 46

Edited by Marianne Krcma